MW00332777

And Finally ...

And Finally ...

A Journalist's Life
in 250 Stories

Paddy Murray

The Liffey Press

Published by
The Liffey Press Ltd
'Clareville'
307 Clontarf Road
Dublin D03 PO46, Ireland
www.theliffeypress.com

© 2021 Paddy Murray

A catalogue record of this book is
available from the British Library.

ISBN 978-1-8383593-0-0

All rights reserved. No part of this publication may be
reproduced or transmitted in any form or by any means,
including photocopying and recording, without written
permission of the publisher. Such written permission must
also be obtained before any part of this publication is stored
in a retrieval system of any nature. Requests for permission
should be directed to The Liffey Press, 'Clareville',
307 Clontarf Road, Dublin D03 PO46, Ireland.

Printed in Spain by GraphyCems.

Contents

Acknowledgements   *xv*

PART 1 – STARTING IN THE MIDDLE . . .

The World of Newspapers   1
The First Assignment   2
The Scoop that Never Saw the Light of Day   4
Another Scoop Missed   6
I Predict a Riot   7
The Big Lie   8
Tragedy   9

Italia '90

The Booze Ban   11
An Irish Solution   12
An Italian Solution   12
A Diplomatic Solution   13
Friends for Ten Minutes   13
The Wall   14
Papal Audience   14
Treated Like Sheep   14
The Brotherhood   15
Home at Last   15
Last Word   16

A Trip Around the World

Four Stories from Montserrat   16
   The Beatles Link   16
   A Slave to the Truth   17
   It Was Bananas   17
   Sunset   18
Australia
   Finally, a Real Scoop   19
   Not Quite Honest   20
   Charlie's Celebration   21
   No Smoke   21
   A Wise Man   22
France   23
Lithuania   23
Belarus   24
Russia   25
South Africa   26
   Repeat Performance   27
Canada   28
United States   29
Thailand   30
Denmark   30
Syria 1990   31

The People One Meets (Part 1)

John Wayne   34
Donovan and Dean Friedman   36
Madonna   36
James Taylor   37
Pele   38
Spike Milligan   38

Contents

Terry Wogan and Brendan Grace   39

J. P. Donleavy   40

Peter Langan   40

Richard Harris   42

Ian Botham   43

Angharad Rees   44

Kim Wilde   45

Elton John   45

Dermot Morgan   48

Jack Charlton   50

Dr Tony O'Neill   52

Eric Clapton   53

George Harrison   54

Gerry Ryan   54

Ray D'Arcy   55

Brendan Grace (again)   56

Tony O'Reilly   57

News Wasn't Always Bad

The Bomb Scare   59

Lou Grant   60

Putting the Boot In   60

A Mother's Advice   61

Me, the Provo   62

A Proper Phone Service   62

Joe Dolan   63

Mickser   63

The Ben Lang   64

A Man of Letters   65

Rocket to the Moon   66

A Good Day for All   66

Keith Wood, Jeremy Guscott and John Pullin   67

And Finally ...

Some Stories That Mattered

The Stardust Fire 68

The Hard Calls 70

Miami Guns 71

JJ 45½ 72

The Whiskey 74

Doug 75

Pandora's Box 77

District Justice James O'Sullivan 79

A Strange Kind of Justice 81

Pure Evil 82

My Brother's Keeper 83

A Lesson Learned 87

Michael and the Aftershave 88

The Mac Stíofáin Hunger Strike 90

Killing Children 91

A Day in Chains 92

The Golden Days 92

Wood Quay 96

Fortuna 97

Slaughter in Fairview 98

The Drinkers Who Become Journalists 99

We're Watching You 100

How a Hangover Cost Me 101

The Secret Talks 101

A Moment I'm Not Proud Of 102

No Daddy for Christmas 102

The Hillsborough Final 103

Becoming an Editor 104

Contents

My Broadcasting Career
(What's the Opposite of Glittering?)

The Talent Show Experience (1) — 106

The Talent Show Experience (2) — 107

The Talent Show Experience (3) — 108

The Lyrics Bored — 108

Line Dancing and Me — 108

A Large Embarrassment — 109

The Pilot Crashes — 109

The Opposite of a Hit Record — 110

The People One Meets (Part 2)

Spandau Ballet and Def Leppard — 111

Charlie Haughey — 112

Barry John — 113

On Murray and Mackey — 114

Albert Reynolds — 115

The Dubliners, The Fureys, Jim McCann
and Stockton's Wing — 117

David Bowie — 119

Johnny Ronan — 120

Fr Brian D'Arcy — 121

Dennis Waterman and Rula Lenska — 122

Ben Bradlee — 123

Phil Orr — 123

Mick Jagger — 124

Laurence Harvey — 125

Lord Henry Mountcharles — 126

Lemmy — 127

Mick McCarthy — 127

Denis Law — 128

Packie Bonner — 129

Michael Schumacher — 129

Steve Bruce and Eric Cantona 130
Shane McGowan 130
Eddie Irvine 131
Harry Crosbie 132
Rosemary Smith 132
Dominic Behan 133
Sir John Leslie 134

Part 2 – Back to the Beginning ...

Spinning Coins 135
A Big Job 135
My Pals 136
Mount Merrion 136
The Church Collection 138
The Accident 139
My Rugby Careeer 140
'Oh Perish Those Who Would So Serious Be' 142
Mr President 143
Frank Left Comedy Behind 143
The 'Millionaires' 144
The Stammer 144
The Brat 145
A Year in Ring 146
JFK in Dublin 148
Dev's Dead 148
No Smoke Without the Nook 149
The Leaving Cert 149
Academics 149
Nicknames 150
Daddy 152
Mammy 156
Lallser 158
My Father and the Famine 159

Contents

Christmas 159

The Fuse 162

The Minister 163

Girlfriends 164

The Scouts 165

The Weddings 166

Life at UCD

Starting Third Level 168

Comedy 168

Michael Collins' Chair 168

The Machine 169

Sniffer Magee 171

Debating and Adrian Hardiman 171

No Standing Upstarts 172

The Hippy 173

Summer Jobs in London, 1972

No Thanks 174

The Crown and Two Chairmen 175

The Sunset Strip 175

De Hems 175

Cockney Pride Tavern 176

Great American Disaster 176

A Tired Girl 177

Further Childhood Adventures

Minerva 179

Dogs 179

Murder 180

The Big Spoof 181

The Pencil 183

The Future Lawyer 184

Fancy Dress 184

PART 3 – MORE FROM THE MIDDLE ...

Six Degrees of Separation

In Australia 185

In South Africa 186

In the Same Band 186

A Shop in Templederry 187

In Templederry Again 187

At the Stables 188

Slow Learner

Figuring It Out (1) 188

Figuring It Out (2) 189

Four Stories about Archibald Albion FC

A Pissed Fullback 191

Hillsborough 2 192

A Case of Mistaken Identity 192

Where's Cardiff? 193

Ten Bits of Very Bad Luck

Missing Out Big Time 193

Fore! 193

Coming Back to Earth 194

Ice Skating Fiasco 194

Look Before You Leap 195

Losing All Sense of Time 196

An Expensive Kick 196

Short-armed 197

Striking Out 198

Missed Out 199

Contents

Ten Stories about Music

VIP   200
Sweet Payback   200
'Do Wah Diddy'   201
The Almost   201
Horslips at Blackrock Park   202
Fleetwood Mac at the National Stadium   203
Calling Radio Luxembourg   204
Some Great Gigs   205
Interviewing Your Hero   205
The Failed Busker   206

Nine Stories Featuring Food

Losing My Appetite   206
Another Lost Customer   207
Daly's Steak House   207
A Drinkin' House   208
Michelin Contender   208
The Friendly House   209
Stung Again   210
One-legged Turkey   211
Welsh Wanker   211

Four Stories about Mirabeau Restaurant

Ditching the Unwelcome   212
Getting Us Home   213
Not the Duck   213
Rolls Royce in Ballymun   213

PART 4 – NEARING THE END ...

Health and Miracles 214
A Kind of Abandonment 221
Winding Down 222
The Cruellest Part 223
God 224
Being Sure 225
Failure and Achievement 225
A World Without 227
Is the Timing Your Choice? 227
My Favourite Word 228
Father's Day 229
Ten Things I Saw that Charlotte Will Never See 230
The Bucket Emptied 232
A Personal Achievement 233
Kevin Street 234
Awards 234
Great Last Words 235

A POSTSCRIPT

Top Twenty of Everything

My Favourite Albums 236
The Best Gigs 237
My Favourite Books 237
The Top Twenty Songs 238
My Favourite Movies 239
My Favourite Pubs in Dublin 240

Acknowledgements

I couldn't, or more accurately wouldn't, have gotten this done without the patience of my wife Connie and daughter Charlotte.

I would also like to thank Brendan 'Beamish' Martin for reminding me of some stories from our great days as a team.

I would like to thank Caroline Mullan, the former archivist in Blackrock College. It was she who, in the first instance, encouraged me, and indeed everybody, to write things down for those who come after us.

And I have to include a special mention for my sister-in-law Ann Kinner, who surprised me with a Christmas present in 2019 of the original rough draft of this memoir which she had printed in book form – a thoughtful gift which spurred me on.

The stories in this book are all true … as far as I can remember. And if they aren't, they should be.

For Connie and Charlotte

Inspired by the courage of Fr Tony Coote

Part 1 – Starting in the Middle . . .

The World of Newspapers

I never planned to be a journalist. In fact, the idea never entered my head.

I was happily working in a dead-end job in London, having failed First Commerce in UCD fairly spectacularly – more of which later – when my brother called to say my mother had managed to get me a place in a journalism course and asked me if I wouldn't mind coming home.

So I did. I don't know why. I never set out to hurt my parents, but obedience wasn't one of my strong points. But home I came and I kind of enjoyed the course and, at the end, a few of us went off to do interviews with the main newspapers as we looked forward to the summer off.

A couple of days after the interviews, a letter arrived offering me a job in the *Independent*. To be honest, I wasn't that interested in taking the job. I had a lazy summer planned.

But my father was interested in me taking the job. That is to say, he was interested in me getting off my backside and actually contributing to life on earth. And so on July 9, 1973, I was packed off on the number 64 bus to my first day working in a proper job, not like the jobs I had been doing in London the summer before when I flitted from bar to strip club to restaurant to bar.

I was greeted that day by Bill Shine, the Chief News Editor and the man who had hired me. I vaguely remember shaking hands with one or two others and was then promptly ignored for about a fortnight!

1

I did get paid though. At the end of the first week I queued up at the cashiers and was handed an envelope containing, after deductions, £17. A fortune. I went off to Brown Thomas and bought a hat, then I bought an LP and I felt kind of pleased with myself. Rich!

When I got home my mother asked me how I got on, admired the hat and asked how much was I going to give towards my keep.

'But you and daddy don't need it,' I protested. 'How much do you want?'

'Five pounds,' she said.

So I handed it to her. And I handed it to her every week for as long as I lived there which was another few years. And when I left, she gave it back, all of it, every penny, telling me it was a lesson.

'Once you start earning, you'll find your money isn't your own.'

And how right she was. Was she right about me and journalism? Pretty much. I got just the 46 years out of it. So far!

What was it like? Like everything else, it has had its ups and downs. And here they are as they popped into my memory.

The First Assignment

And so it began. It was July 1973 when, as a 19-year-old raw recruit out of college for just a few weeks, I was offered a job in Independent Newspapers. It lasted 46 years.

Back then the newsroom wasn't set up to train new reporters. The concept of interns was many years away. And so, for the first few weeks, I dutifully arrived into the office at 8.00 am, ostensibly to work on the *Evening Herald*. I sat in front of a typewriter, read newspapers, responded to the few who said hello and then, at 4.30, I went home.

It was a month after my arrival in the newsroom that I finally got to write a story. And it was a big one.

I will always remember August 3, 1973, two days before my twentieth birthday. It was that day I was sent out of the office on what was a major story. It was absolutely by chance that I was sent on the job. Had there been an alternative, I would have been left sitting at my silent typewriter.

But on that morning I was the only 'reporter' in the newsroom when the story broke. The news editor, Padraig Beirne, looked around in vain for a more senior reporter, a real reporter, anyone but the kid at the back of the room. But the first edition of the *Herald* was gone so they were all on their mid-morning breaks, some for coffee, a few for something stronger.

They were out of contact – it was long before mobile phones or take away coffee – so he looked down towards me.

'Young fella,' he said, not actually knowing my name.

I went to the desk and received instructions to head out to Crumlin where a man had been shot in a payroll robbery. And off I went, blue docket in hand to pay the taxi driver, biro and notebook in my pocket.

When I got to the scene, there were gardaí everywhere and locals who had gathered to watch the aftermath of the robbery. I decided to approach one of them, a young, scruffy lad in jeans and t-shirt. But when I asked him what happened he said, in a gruff rural accent, 'You'll have to get on to the Garda Press Office,' thereby blowing his cover.

I managed to talk to a few locals who had arrived on the scene shortly after the robbery and they told me what happened, or what they heard had happened – I got the story.

A man called James Farrell had been shot dead and another man injured as they brought cash for a payroll to a local business. The robbery (though we didn't know it at the time) was the work of the IRA.

I wrote the story and managed to persuade a woman living near the scene to let me use her phone. It turned out that she had the only phone in the immediate neighbourhood, and I remember her standing right beside me as I filed my story. I was nervous. But I was relatively happy with what I had sent in.

Nobody said much when I got back. There were a few withering looks which seemed to suggest, to me anyway, that there was a view a kid shouldn't have been sent on such a big story. Then the paper came up from the press. It was the lead story, of course. I don't think my name was on it. But that didn't matter at the time.

Padraig looked down towards me and signalled me to come to his desk. It would take another week or so for him to get my name.

'See how the *Press* did it?'

I looked. The *Evening Press* had the name of the dead man wrong. I looked at Padraig.

'You did well,' he said almost, but not quite, smiling. He didn't call me Paddy. But he didn't call me young fella again either.

And I had got it right. I walked away from Padraig feeling quite smug. Paddy Murray, reporter.

The Scoop that Never Saw the Light of Day

It seems that the border will always be a topic of conversation on our island. In recent years, because of Brexit, we've talked about hard borders and soft borders. In a way, it was always thus.

Roy Bradford was a Unionist politician and at one time a minister in the North. Way, way back in the 1970s, he made a speech in Dublin. He made it in, of all places, the Knights of Columbanus headquarters in Ely Place. Yes, indeed. A Unionist made a speech in the headquarters of a very Catholic organisation.

It was supposed to be a private affair. But I knew a man who worked there so I managed to sneak in and sit at the back. And I listened in amazement as Mr Bradford told the audience of Southern Catholics that he thought a United Ireland was inevitable. And not only was it inevitable, he didn't think it would be entirely a bad thing. In fact, he thought Unionists might eventually embrace the idea. Lordy God, I thought, I have a scoop. So I went back to the office – no mobiles back then – and wrote the story.

There was a degree of amazement because this kid had this extraordinary story. It was decided to run it past Conor O'Brien, the editor, to see just how big we'd go on it. He called me into his office. I presumed it was to congratulate me. After all, this was Conor 'News' O'Brien, the man who had the courage to run Joe McAnthony's expose of the Irish Sweepstakes just a few years earlier. But there was no congratulations.

'We can't run the story,' he said.

I didn't understand. So he explained.

'I had lunch with Roy Bradford today and I promised him we wouldn't report on his speech. I gave my word,' he said. 'That's the only reason he felt he could say what he said.'

I was crestfallen. I was also too young and naïve to realise that, given its importance, I should have given the story to another newspaper or to RTÉ, even if it meant being disloyal to my employer. But I didn't.

It does go to show, though, that even fifty years or more ago, when the North was ablaze, things weren't quite as carved in stone as we thought they were.

Another Scoop Missed

I was dispatched to Mullaghmore in County Sligo on August 27, 1979 to report back on the murder of Lord Mountbatten, Baroness Brabourne, Lord Mountbatten's grandson Nicholas Knatchbull and young Paul Maxwell.

It was a difficult workplace. Security was very, very tight. Information was scarce. We were left, essentially, writing colour, which is what we journalists call a piece of descriptive text that paints a picture but can be short on actual facts. Sometimes, it's your imagination that saves you on a story like that.

So I asked a senior garda if it was possible that the bomb which killed the elderly pair and the young boys could have been placed in a lobster pot and detonated as they passed.

'Unlikely,' he said.

I asked again if it was possible.

'Can't see it,' he said.

So I asked once more.

'Look,' he said, 'it's just not likely, not the way the IRA works, not on our radar. Possible? Remotely.'

That was good enough for me. And so the *Herald* led with the story of the Lobster Pot Bomb.

The following day, the same garda came to me, quietly, and asked me why I 'ran with that shit'.

I told him I had to run something.

'But I told you we already had the bastards who did it. I told you they were actually arrested *before* the fuckin' bomb went off,' he said.

He was referring to the arrest of Thomas McMahon and Francis McGirl. A suspicious garda, knowing their association with the IRA, had stopped and arrested them 70 miles from the explosion as the bomb went off. McMahon had flakes of paint

6

from the Mountbatten boat and nitroglycerin on his clothes. He served 30 years for his crime. McGirl was acquitted.

'You didn't tell me that,' I said.

'Well, fuck it, I meant to,' he said, and walked away.

He meant to.

And because he didn't, I missed my biggest scoop. *Ever!*

I Predict a Riot

It was July 18, 1981 and the Hunger Strikes in the North were causing distress and political mayhem. By that date six prisoners, including Bobby Sands, had died, so there was bound to be nervousness around the march planned for Dublin that day.

It was to go from the city centre to the British Embassy in Ballsbridge, the one which replaced the embassy on Merrion Square which burned down after the Bloody Sunday killings. I was on the newsdesk for the *Herald* that day. And Liam Collins was the senior reporter covering the march.

This wasn't the era of the internet. We had to plan and get our stories as early as we could. So the first edition went off without much mention of the march. We needed something for the later editions. No point just saying it took place. We needed to know what happened.

At around midday, Liam called in from a phone box along the route. They had only reached Nassau Street and had a couple of miles yet to go to reach the embassy. No trouble. A brick thrown at a British-owned shop, that was the height of it. I asked Liam what was going to happen.

'There's going to be a riot,' he said. 'Some are marching with baseball bats and pick axe handles. There will be trouble.'

I asked him if he was sure. He said he was.

I asked him if we should run a story saying there was a riot. He said we should.

And so he wrote a story about the riot which had erupted outside the British embassy in Ballsbridge. Only he wrote it and I sent it for printing an hour before it actually happened. In fact, there's a chance the paper came out of the printworks on Prince's Street a few minutes before a pick axe handle was swung or a stone thrown in anger in Ballsbridge.

But we had the story. It was on our front page so when the rioters came back into the city centre, it was all there. When people out in the suburbs bought their papers at six o'clock, we had the details. Sometimes, you have to take risks.

The Big Lie

Only once did I ever completely fabricate a story for a newspaper.

I had been sent to the Cheltenham races to write a diary for the *Evening Herald*. I have no interest in horse racing and I don't think I've ever enjoyed a race meeting in my life. Too many people rushing about, banging into each other, trying for better odds or looking for (what they think are) tips and so on. Cheltenham for a week was, for me, hell.

Anyway, I had managed not to see a horse and it was day three. It was going well. But, frankly, I was running out of stuff to write. I had already, with the help of colleagues, identified and written about everyone there who was famous or vaguely so. And now, the page was blank.

'The Queen Mother is arriving,' someone said behind me.

Great, I thought. One line. And then I thought, hold on. You see, Ireland's preeminent racing commentator, Michael O'Hehir, had just fallen ill with a stroke. He was missing Cheltenham. And, for years, he and Cheltenham week had been synonymous. A light bulb went on over my head.

First, though, I did check one thing. That the Queen Mum had actually arrived.

I went out and saw her walk into the posh part of the grandstand. I waved, she waved back – well, that's my story – and I retreated to the press tent where I wrote:

'The Queen Mother breezed into Cheltenham yesterday, and the first question she asked was, "How is Michael O'Hehir?"'

Cracking story which would have been even better if it had been true. Anyway, the *Herald* ran with it. My colleagues asked me how I had got the story. I told them the truth. I made it up.

'But...' they began.

'Do you think the Palace will deny it? Do you think they're going to come out and say she *didn't* ask for Michael O'Hehir?'

And to cap it all, the next day *three* English newspapers ran the story having lifted it from the *Herald*. Vindication!

Tragedy

It was November 13, 1984. I had been out with friends in the Mirabeau restaurant in Sandycove, probably the only posh or showbizzy restaurant in Dublin at the time. We had our meal and adjourned to the Zhivago nightclub off Baggot Street. It was owned by a friend, Pat Gibbons. I went to the bar to order a few bottles of wine for us – my former wife Paula and our friends Frank and Mary Slattery from Tralee. I heard one of the girls behind the bar mention my colleague, John Feeney.

'You're not saying anything bad about John,' I said with a smile.

'You haven't heard have you?' she said. 'Go and sit down. I'll bring some wine over.'

I returned to our table and remarked that the waitress was behaving very oddly. She came over and sat down. She poured some wine.

'John is dead,' she said.

I thought it was a joke.

'I'm sorry,' she said. 'The plane crashed.'

The plane. I knew John had been on 'the Beaujolais Run' as we called it. I had done it the year before. It was, essentially, a press junket. Over to Paris on a small plane to pick up a bottle of Beaujolais Nouveau and back again on the same night.

But then it dawned on me that my editor and friend Niall Hanley was also on the trip. And my colleagues Kevin Marron and Tony Heneghan. I couldn't take it in. If the plane had crashed they were all dead. I called the office.

It was even worse. Pat Gibbons, in whose club I sat, was dead too along with restaurateur Francois Schelbaum. And Cormac Cassidy from Cassidy wines. And Arrigo Chichi. They were all men I knew to a greater or lesser degree. The pilot was an experienced flier called Jack Walsh. I told the others I had to go.

I got to the office where there was a stunned silence. I was, at the time, Assistant Editor of the *Herald*. And then my friend Deputy Editor James Morrissey arrived. We decided to go to Niall's house. There were a few there before us as we sympathised with his widow June and young children Barrie and Helen. We stayed a while. But as we left, either one or the other of us suddenly realised that we had work to do.

It was three or four in the morning when we got back to the office. John Feeney had filed earlier and there were two pages by him in the *Herald*, due on the streets in about eight hours. Kevin Marron's column filled another page.

James and I sat at a desk in the middle of the room and, together, wrote four obituaries. They were tear-filled, sentimental and anything but journalistic. But we had both done something essential, something professional, something Niall would have been proud of. We kept the show on the road.

Italia '90

There had never been a time like it before and there hasn't been one since. We had won Olympic gold medals, Triple Crowns, we'd had magnificent All Ireland Finals, world champions in boxing and Tour de France winners. But nothing came close to Italia '90, which seems like a lifetime ago now. We had reached the last eight in the world and the team arrived home to a street party which outdid all street parties!

But it wasn't just on the pitch that the fun was had. I spent five weeks in Italy with the fans. Here are some of my memories.

The Booze Ban

There was (an attempted) Booze Ban. It was forbidden to sell alcohol immediately before or after the games. And so, when I arrived late for lunch in Cagliari the day of the English game, I was resigned to having a glass of water with my food. My colleagues were already at the table. A waiter arrived. He was holding a large Coke bottle and a large 7 Up bottle.

'Would you like Coke or 7 Up?' he asked.

I told him I wanted neither. He asked again and again. I kept saying no. My colleagues were smiling. The waiter leaned towards me and whispered the question.

'Would you like *red* Coke or *white* 7 Up?'

I had the red Coke.

An Irish Solution

In Palermo, we went into a bar one evening during the Booze Ban. It was packed. Half the customers were Irish, half were locals. They weren't hiding. It was noisy. There was singing. I got myself a drink and sidled up to one of the locals.

'Why don't the police shut this bar like they've shut the others? I asked.

'Because we *are* the police,' came the reply.

It felt like home.

An Italian Solution

Then, the morning after the night before – or rather the lunchtime after the night before – I made my way to the bar in our hotel in Palermo. I ordered a Bloody Mary. I sat down with some of the other lads. They laughed.

'What good is a Bloody Mary without the vodka?' they asked.

But I distinctly remember the barman putting vodka in the drink. And I told them so.

'You imagined it,' they said. 'We tried all sorts to get him to give us a drink but he said no, he couldn't.'

So I went up to the bar. They followed. I can't remember his name – we knew him well at the time! – but I called the barman over and asked him if there was vodka in the Bloody Mary.

'Of course,' he said.

One of the other lads looked at him. 'But what about the Booze Ban?' he asked.

'This is not booze,' he said lifting my Bloody Mary, 'this is food.'

It was Bloody Marys all around.

A Diplomatic Solution

The night before the Italian match in Rome, there was a gang of us in a pub, singing and drinking. A cop came in.

'No singing,' he said. 'The American ambassador lives nearby. He says you are noisy. He must sleep. No singing.'

He left. We stopped singing. For ten minutes. Then we started again. The cop came in again. We stopped again. Then we sang again. Then he arrived in looking angry. He was holding his baton in one hand and banging it into the palm of the other. He was looking very serious.

'The American ambassador,' he said, 'wants to know if you will sing "Danny Boy".'

So we did.

Friends for Ten Minutes

I was chatting to a couple of Irish fans on the street in Cagliari on June 11, 1990, when two English lads approached. It had just been announced on a Tannoy that there were more tickets available to be purchased at the station. The English lads told us they went to buy tickets but were refused because they were English. They wanted to borrow two shirts of the Irish lads. No problem.

'Do you want our shirts while we're away?' the English lads asked.

'Eh, no,' was the response.

Fifteen minutes later the English lads were back with their tickets. They took off the Irish shirts and handed them back.

'Thanks lads. Brilliant. Love the Irish fans. Really grateful,' one of the English lads said.

'Gascoigne is a wanker,' came the response.

Normal service was resumed.

The Wall

There was the story of The Wall in Cagliari too. Now, I've been accused of making this up but I didn't. I was told it by someone and choose to believe it. The story goes like this.

A hot afternoon in Sardinia. Irish lads in a campsite are watching an Italian builder working on a new wall. It's afternoon so he takes his 'siesta'. The job was half done. The Irish lads looked at each other, nodded, and finished the wall to the surprise of the builder when he returned.

Well, the way things were going in Italy that summer, it probably was true!

Papal Audience

The only team granted an audience with Pope John Paul II was Ireland. A few fans and a few hacks like myself were present when the Pontiff greeted the team and walked along the line to shake hands with Jack and each of the players. It was probably the only time a football song was sung in the Vatican. As the Pope greeted the players, the fans – very gently – broke into 'We're All Part of Jackie's Army.'

Treated Like Sheep

There was deep worry in Cagliari about Irish and English fans mixing before the game. The reputation of English fans had not been enhanced by the behaviour of a few in Germany two years previously. And so it was thought the Irish fans were in danger.

When the famous cruise ship the *Achille Lauro* – it had been the subject of hijacking some years earlier – docked carrying hundreds of Irish fans, the port gates were locked. Armed police stood outside as the Irish fans stood on the quayside in sweltering heat. The stand-off went on and on. The cops didn't look like they were going to open the gate. And then ... and then one fan bleated. 'Baaa Baaaa.'

Silence.

Then two or three did it. 'Baaa. Baaa. Baaa.' Then ten. Then forty. Then they whole damned lot. The cops smiled. Then they laughed and opened the gate.

The Brotherhood

In fairness to the FAI, they did everything they could to source tickets for the thousands of fans who turned up for the match against Romania in Genoa. And they had to deal with some unsavoury characters. I met one FAI official who told me he had just had an extraordinary experience.

'I was looking for a colleague so I knocked on a door upstairs in the hotel because I'd been told he might be at a meeting there. I went in. There he was at one end of the table. Three Italian guys in suits were at the other end. The table was covered in tickets and money. I wasn't sure how to handle it, so I dragged up my *cúpla focal*.

"Cé hiad sin?" I asked him.

"Na madraí," he replied.

So I left them at it.'

Home at Last

Finally, one I didn't see – but it is true.

The Irish team arrived home to a hero's welcome on July 1, 1990. But earlier that day, Nelson Mandela had arrived at the airport. When he did, it was already packed with Irish fans awaiting the arrival of Jack and the lads. The fans were decent enough to cheer Mandela when he stepped out of the plane. Maybe he presumed they were there for him. It was all very dignified until...

One voice again. And then they all joined in. 'Ohh ah, it's Paul McGrath's da, Ooh ah, it's Paul McGrath's da.'

Last Word

We won that World Cup. Oh you might say Italy beat us in Rome. Maybe they did. But we still won it.

A Trip Around the World

Four Stories from Montserrat

The Beatles Link

It was during the 1980s that I was sent off to the Caribbean island of Montserrat. It was to do a story about how they celebrated St Patrick's Day. It was, after all, known as the Emerald Isle of the Caribbean. It was a stunningly beautiful place. The airport was, effectively, a beach which had been concreted over. Customs consisted of a guy, sitting outdoors on the 'beach' with a table on which were papers held down by stones. He asked us – I was with photographer Frank McGrath Jnr – where we were from, how long we were staying, what we were doing and then:

'What kind of music are you into?'

It was that kind of place. I met many of the locals who had Irish names and an old man who spoke with an Irish accent though he had never left the island. I got to spend some time in the Air Studios owned by Sir George Martin, the man who made the Beatles. It was at these studios where Elton John, Dire Straits, The Police, Paul McCartney, The Rolling Stones and so many others recorded albums. Indeed, Midge Ure was on the island at the time.

Yvonne Kelly ran the place. When I called and asked if we could visit she said we could, but she could only let us stay 15

16

minutes. We stayed for hours. I asked her about the 15 minutes thing.

'I say that to all journalists who visit. It means that if they're assholes I can tell them their 15 minutes is up. You're not assholes. Stay as long as you like!'

A Slave to the Truth

The island was and is very Irish. Their passport stamp was a shamrock, and St Patrick's Day was their national day. Only...

Well, I had been talking to this historian about the island's links with Ireland and he didn't seem terribly enthusiastic about telling me too much. He wasn't rude, just reticent. Eventually, I asked him once too often I suppose.

'Right,' he said. 'You want to know so I'm going to tell you. When Irish Catholics were driven out of the southern United States, they came here. And they became the worst, most nasty, most cruel slave masters there has ever been. Every St Patrick's Day, they got drunk and so on March 17th, 1768 the slaves tried to take advantage of their drunk masters and staged a revolt. They didn't win, but that's why it's the national holiday!'

Right then. That put me in my box!

Anyway, on July 18, 1995, Montserrat's Soufrière Hills volcano, which had been dormant for centuries, erupted burying the capital Plymouth in volcanic dust. Most islanders left and half is still unpopulated.

It Was Bananas

I think the climate on the island just might have been conducive to the growing of some crops if not others. I met a man on the quay who had clearly been smoking some weed. I said hello, and then noticed that bananas were being unloaded from a ship in the port.

'You import bananas?' I said to him.

'Yeh man,' he said, giving me a clue as to what he might be smoking.

'Would you not grow them here?' I asked.

He looked shocked. 'Grow them? No way man. You'd have to plant them and look after them and pick them.' And he strolled off.

Probably explained too why most of the shops in the then capital, Plymouth, closed if a cruise ship pulled in. But it was a wonderful place.

Sunset

Yes, I was so lucky to be sent to Montserrat in the West Indies to file stories about its Irishness and why the people celebrated St Patrick's Day as their national holiday. While there, I called the governor's residence and I was invited to visit. It was a fine building with a shamrock over the veranda, which overlooked the Caribbean.

So I sat down with the governor and we chatted. And we had a few drinks. Quite a few. And I think he might have had quite a few more than I.

He told me that he loved the place and that he had little to do in reality. It was a lovely climate, lovely people, lovely place. And as the sun began to go down and a kind of dusk settled around us, my new friend the governor turned to me and, in a slightly slurred voice, said:

'You know, they think they punished me by sending me here...'

Australia

Finally, a Real Scoop

Back in the late 1980s, Gay Byrne announced that he would be broadcasting his radio show from Sydney, Australia in a few weeks' time. I was in Tralee covering the annual Rose Festival and having a few jars now and then (or was it having a few jars and covering the Rose Festival now and then?). My then boss at the *Evening Herald*, Michael Brophy, called me and asked me to have a word with Gay who was, as ever, hosting the event on television.

'Ask him, if I was to send you out to Australia with him, if he would co-operate with us doing stories every day.'

I did. He said he would. And so off I went to Australia.

It was all a bit rushed and I was absolutely knackered by the time I landed. I got into bed to recover from the jet lag. The phone rang. It was Gaybo's producer John Caden, telling me they had a great story. The show's production team had already been in Sydney for a few days.

'Yeh, yeh,' I replied. I said I was tired and needed sleep. I said I'd call back later. Then he called again telling me Gay wanted to talk to me. Well, not many journalists get a call telling them Gay Byrne wants to talk to them. So I struggled out of bed and…

I got up to John's room and he was in bed. Gay and some other members of the team were there. John started to tell me the story. It seems that they had all gone out to Bondi Beach that morning. Three of them, John, Philip Kampf and Cathy Moore, went for a swim. They waved at Gay from the sea. All jolly good fun. Well, it was until Gay realised they weren't happy waves.

The three of them were in trouble and they were waving to attract attention so Gay could raise the alarm. They were being swept out to sea by a 'rip', a strong current almost invisible to the naked eye. All three had to be rescued by a lifeguard who, despite the fact that Cathy was the strongest swimmer, rescued her first. Well, she was a lot better looking than John or Philip – at least that was his excuse.

The story of the dramatic rescue of Gay Byrne's team on Bondi Beach was, of course, a massive lead story for the *Evening Herald*. The then editor of the *Evening Press*, Sean Ward, told me later that it was the only time he had ever been caught completely cold by a story. And that made it all the better!

Not Quite Honest

Well, I was still knackered the following day. I was lying in bed in the early evening, reading a local newspaper, when the phone rang. It was Michael Brophy.

'Could you go to a local supermarket and get the prices of everyday produce? We want to compare them with prices here. You have an hour.'

It wasn't a request. I cursed him. I was absolutely shattered. But I didn't have a choice. I turned the page in the newspaper, half subconsciously, and lo and behold, what was on the two pages I opened up? A massive ad for a local supermarket with the price of bread and eggs and milk and butter and meat and wine and cheese and vegetables and, well, everything. I lay back on the bed for 45 minutes and then I called Michael.

'Damn you,' I said. I was half asleep when you rang but, look, I went out and got those prices for you.'

So I filed my story. I'm sure Michael thought I was a real pro for knuckling down and getting the job done. So did I!

Charlie's Celebration

There was also actual work involved in the trip. One job was interviewing a man called Gary Foley, a spokesman for the Aborigines, and an obvious question, I thought, was about his surname. Where did the 'Foley' come from?

'My ancestors were owned by Foleys,' he said. Right.

He spoke about the treatment of his fellow Aborigines over the years. And then he asked me if it was true that Charlie Haughey was planning to visit the Australia Bicentennial later that year. I told him it was.

'Ask him why he's coming here to celebrate 200 years of British colonisation,' Gary said.

I didn't ask. I just wrote it.

No Smoke

I was persuaded, during the Sydney trip, to visit a friend of a friend. She lived in the suburbs with her husband. I knew neither of them beforehand. We ate a bit, drank a few beers and then, when his wife was out of the room, the husband asked me if I'd like to share a joint. I said I would.

So we went into the back garden and he lit the joint and told me that if his wife asked, we just went out for a smoke. I got a nice buzz. At first. And then I could feel my heart pounding. I mean, really pounding and racing. I told him so. His first concern? His wife.

'Don't tell her we smoked a joint,' he said. 'I'll call you a cab.'

And that's what he did as my pulse raced and raced.

'What did I smoke?' I asked him.

'Eh, Thai sticks. Should've said,' he muttered.

My flight was that night. I got on the plane and slept all the way home. The next day I went to my doctor and told him what happened. He said I was lucky.

'If you'd come to me here with the symptoms you describe, I would have called an ambulance, not a taxi.'

A Wise Man

I met a man called Tony Onions during that Sydney trip. Fascinating guy. He asked if I'd like to ride a horse around a property in which he had an interest. Sounded like a great idea.

'That's an interesting way to spend my last day here,' I said.

'Last day?' he said back. 'Nah. It would be pointless. It would take three days to ride around the place.'

'How big is it?' I asked.

'A million acres,' he said.

Ireland is 21,500,000 acres! Still, it would have been safer than those damned Thai sticks.

Tony was very wise. Originally from the Irish midlands, he had been living in Australia for some time. We spoke about the Irish who have moved there. And some who moved there and then returned home.

'If you emigrate, you need to stop looking over your shoulder. That's the problem many of the Irish here have,' he said. 'They arrive and spend their time wondering what's going on at home. Those Irish lessons in Sydney? Why didn't they learn Irish in Ireland? It's just homesickness. And do you know what happens? They come here, they think of home all the time and they go home. And what do they do there? Wonder what it would have been like if they had stayed here!'

Tony was much loved. He lived in a place called Marulan with his wife Jean Ranken of Lockyersleigh. Tony loved Marulan and worked enthusiastically to improve the town and help the residents. After he died in 1989, not so long after my Australian visit, the Marulan residents named their local park in appreciation of Tony's work and love of the area.

France

I can't even remember the year. But I was in Paris for the rugby and I hooked up with Liam Collins. A dangerous thing to do. We of course went to the match. And then we went on the piss. We bumped into a load of Irish after the game and gave it a lash, but at about eight or nine o'clock someone suggested food.

John McColgan had recommended a restaurant to me before we left Dublin so that's where we went. It was called, I believe, Les Balkans. It wasn't that busy. So we asked if they could accommodate, I think it was around 14 of us.

'We are about to close, main course only,' a waiter told us sternly.

I was a bit embarrassed having brought a gang of people to the place. But we sat down. A waiter was summoned.

'May we order some wine?'

He nodded his assent.

'What do you want?' he asked.

The person ordering looked around and counted.

'I think 12 bottles of red and two white.'

I don't think they'd ever seen anything like it. We ate at least three courses and, naturally, had a few more rounds of wine. It was after two o'clock when we finished, paid the bill and left a generous tip. And the head waiter, the one who had told us we could only have one course, said that if any of us wanted a lift back to our hotel, his staff would be more than willing to drive us. The offer was, of course, accepted.

Lithuania

I was a regular in Eastern Europe for a while. We had games in Latvia, Lithuania and Poland and not only did I have to attend the matches, I had, in the weeks preceding the games, to travel to these countries to write preview pieces for the fans who would be traveling and, indeed, for those we weren't going to be able to make the trip.

When I made the preview trips, I generally travelled alone. And so, on one occasion, I was flying from Vilnius, capital of Lithuania, to Warsaw, capital of Poland. I checked in, went through security, and walked to the plane. It held about 34 passengers.

The first thing that struck me when I boarded was that despite the fact that the plane was being refuelled, several passengers were smoking. With the door open. And the cabin crew watching. I didn't like it.

Eventually the cigarettes were put out and we were told – at least I presume we were told because I didn't understand a word of the announcements – to prepare for departure. Then, just before they closed the door, six or seven passengers rushed on. There were no seats for them. Two walked straight into the cockpit. Five stood for the entire flight which lasted just over an hour or, in my case, a lifetime. I ran off the plane as soon as it landed.

Belarus

I have no idea why I was in Belarus. On a coach. With Irish football fans. I can only surmise that it had something to do with playing Latvia and Lithuania a week apart in the 1993

World Cup qualifiers. I suspect we were on our way to Moscow for a few days.

It was a very, very boring trip. Out the windows of the bus we could see grim apartment blocks and grim factories as we entered the city of Minsk. Occasionally it would be grim factories and grim apartment blocks. Then our guide – really, there was a guide – told us we were approaching something which was very, very exciting. He urged us to look out the windows on the left (where, at the time, all we could see were grim factories and grim apartment blocks).

'We are getting closer,' he said.

We wondered what it could be.

And then he said: 'There, there it is.'

We looked, but all we could see were the aforementioned grim etc. We still wondered. And then he ended the suspense.

'There, up on the hill. That is the biggest washing machine factory in the world!'

I started thinking about Newgrange and the Empire State and the Louvre and St Mark's Square. Nah. This was the real thing. A washing machine factory.

Russia

After the excitement of Belarus, I visited the Russian city of Pskov. Pskov is close to Estonia so me and a few fans booked into a hotel there. It had to be value for money!

Our train was late getting to Pskov so I was a bit anxious about getting my stuff across in time for the next day's paper. It was a Sunday and Monday was a big sports day so stuff about the games and the fans and the places we were visiting was important.

When we got to the hotel I rushed up to the reception and said, 'I am a journalist. I need to make an urgent call to Dublin, Ireland.'

The receptionist said it was no problem. She would make the arrangements and come up to my room to let me know when it was all in order. I waited anxiously in my room. It was getting really late in Ireland. About half an hour later, there was a knock on the door. It was the receptionist.

'I have arranged your call to Dublin,' she said. 'I told them it was very important.'

'Thank God,' I replied. 'When can I make it?'

'Wednesday,' she said, looking very pleased with herself.

'Eh, but I need to make a call now,' I protested.

'Oh no. It usually takes more than a week to book a foreign call,' she said. 'I did very well to get Wednesday.'

And she went on her way. First and only time I failed to file.

South Africa

The Rugby World Cup in South Africa in 1995 was a brilliant experience. As ever, I travelled alone though I managed to hook up with some familiar and some unfamiliar faces during the tournament. There was drink involved much of the time, your honour.

A bunch of us decided, one day, to go on a bus trip around the Cape. It was the least we could do having flown thousands of miles to get there. Off we went and as we travelled our guide pointed out sights which were a great deal more interesting and beautiful than washing machine factories. After a couple of hours, the coach stopped.

We were in a lovely small town called Fish Hoek and it looked just like the kind of place we could go for a stroll or just wander around looking at the sights and, well, maybe have a drink. We all checked our stuff and got ready to disembark.

'One thing,' the driver said then. 'This is a dry town.'

He was right. The sun was shining and there wasn't a cloud in the sky. And then it dawned on us. He meant dry. As in alcohol-free.

'There is a long tradition in Fish Hoek that no alcohol is permitted in the town.'

He looked around. Nobody was budging.

'We have about an hour or so here,' he said.

Nobody moved. And then somebody spoke up and said, 'Drive on'.

We all mumbled agreement.

'But...' he tried to no avail.

'Drive on. We've seen it.'

And so he did.

Repeat Performance

We were staying in Sun City for part of our trip. It was expensive. But of course, I wasn't paying!

So when we enquired about doing a hot air balloon over a safari park and heard the price was over £100, some squirmed. But I didn't. It was the only thing on the whole trip I paid for out of my own pocket. And what a trip.

Our American pilot took us up and over the park. We saw everything. Elephants, rhinos, hippos, lions – the works. It was fantastic. And then we were told it was time to land. But as we descended, the pilot seemed to panic.

'Please, everyone, sit there facing away from the direction we're travelling in. Backs to the basket. Now.'

So we did.

'Brace yourselves. We're going to clip that tree...'

We could hear the branches scraping along the bottom of the balloon's basket. But we landed safely, relieved and happy. I collected a few to give to the pilot. I handed the money to him and he thanked me.

'Can I ask one question?' I said.

'Sure thing Paddy,' he said.

'Do you always clip the tree?'

He looked away. He looked back. He was smiling.

'We always clip the tree,' he said. 'Part of the show!'

It was still brilliant.

Canada

I ended up in Toronto with my colleague Ronan Farren. Don't know who paid the bill but I do know it was a junket of some sort. We were each to write a travel piece on our return.

We stayed in an apartment in central Toronto. So naturally, we dumped our bags and looked for a bar. We found one, downtown in an area we later discovered was a kind of business zone.

We went into the first bar we saw and I ordered two beers. When they were consumed, Ronan ordered two more. Then I ordered two more. And then it was Ronan's turn. The barman looked at him disapprovingly.

'You guys have already had three.'

God almighty, Ronan and I often had six or seven in the Horse and Tram. We left.

Next day, instead of turning left to go down town, we turned right up to the university area. Good move. We went into a bar and it was humming. So we felt comfortable having our, eh, few beers. Then a little mixed group came in. Students we presumed. One of them went to the bar.

'Four Beam Me Up Scottys please', he said.

28

I can't remember if the barman knew what it contained or whether we asked. But it was a shot of Coffee liqueur, a shot of Baileys and a shot of banana liqueur, served in a glass as three stripes. Each of the party sat and looked at their drink. Then it was down in one. Same guy went to the bar again.

'Four Beam Me Up Scottys please.'

And then he got four more. It was about 40 minutes later when he approached the bar for his fourth and last time.

'Four Bream me up Schottees pleash.'

He got them, the group downed them and they left. I cannot imagine how our downtown barman would have reacted.

United States

My first trip to New York was in 1980. I had arrived equipped with the warning that New Yorkers were direct. They said what they meant but meant no harm by it. I wasn't quite sure what to take from that warning.

Anyway, a place I had to see on that first trip was Macy's. So I wandered in and when I went in to the men's department saw a sign. Calvin Klein Valise only $10 with any Calvin Klein male cosmetic purchase.

Let me set the scene. I'm looking at the sign. I had long hair. I was wearing a t-shirt and jeans. I wasn't what you would call a typical Macy's customer of the time.

So I walked up to the counter behind which a woman in her fifties was standing. She looked me up and down. And before I had the chance to say a word, she spoke:

'The cheapest item we have is the soap,' she said firmly.

So I bought the second cheapest.

Thailand

I was on a junket with a few British journalists. There were four men and a woman on the trip. We weren't in our hotel five minutes when two guys from the British travel company which brought us phoned our rooms and invited us to join them in reception. When I say 'us', I mean the men. So we did. And they invited us to join them in the back of a limousine which sped off through Bangkok to its destination.

We arrived at a modest three or four storey building. We went in. There was what looked like a bar on the left on the ground floor but we were ushered up to the second floor. There, behind a glass partition, sat about a dozen girls ranging in age from, I'd say, 15 to18. Each had a number on her wrist.

'Welcome to Bangkok. Our treat,' said one of our hosts.

We stood there. And then I spoke.

'I don't know if it's my Catholic upbringing or it's because I have a wife at home, I don't know if it's fear of catching something or maybe it's because they're children, but if you don't mind, I saw a bar on the way in and I'll be there when you're all finished.'

And I walked out. I walked up to the bar and heard a voice behind me. Two of the three other journalists stood there.

'Thanks,' they both said. 'Not sure we could have put it so well.'

Okay. One hack did what he did. But there was silence as we were dropped back to our hotel. And we never saw our 'hosts' again.

Denmark

Queen Margrethe of Denmark was planning a state visit to Ireland. So a few random hacks were brought over to Denmark to learn about and, presumably, appreciate all things Danish before their Queen paid us a visit. We were brought here and there and treated like, well, royalty. And we survived one of our number who just couldn't resist stirring it a few times. I will only say that he was a Corkman!

We went to the ballet. Now, it's not my favourite form of entertainment but we were guests of the Danish government and royal family so two hours of ballet seemed to be a small price to pay. It ended. And one of our hosts asked how we enjoyed it. I mumbled something about it being magnificent. My Cork colleague went further.

'In the first half, the guy in front of me leaned to one side so I could only see half the stage,' he said.

'Oh that's a pity,' said our host. 'I hope it was different after the interval.'

'It was,' my colleague said. 'He moved out of the way so unfortunately I could see the whole damned thing.'

He was rewarded with a weak smile.

Next day, we were given the tour of the Carlsberg brewery. They're very proud of it. When the tour was over, we were all asked what we thought of it. And of course, we all said it was brilliant. Well, all except my Cork friend.

'It was lovely. Like Guinness. Only smaller.'

They weren't impressed.

Syria 1990

Jim Walpole and I weren't long back from Italia '90 when we were sent away again. It seems that it was generally held that we had done a good job so we were given a difficult assignment as a reward. This time, it wasn't to be so glamorous. Damascus. We were sent there because the rumour was that Brian Keenan was about to be released after his long time in captivity.

31

It didn't start well. Jim sailed through the airport as did most of the other journalists who arrived. I, and a couple of others, were told to sit and wait. So we sat and waited for hours and hours and hours. When we went to the toilet, we were accompanied by armed guards. Intimidation seemed to be the aim of the exercise. I got fed up.

I asked to speak with someone in charge and eventually someone in uniform turned up and started bullshitting about visas and so on. I told him I wasn't interested. I told him I had a visa but if it wasn't the right one that was grand. Just get me on the next flight out and you can then explain to your minister, at whose invitation we are there, why we left. What time can I go? He let us out. We had been in the airport, sitting on benches, for 24 hours.

Anyway, out we were and ready to do a spot of work. Sadly, the advice from an Irish Army officer stationed in Damascus to eat 'nothing that comes out of the ground because of what it's fertilised with' (i.e. human excrement) came too late for Jim who fell seriously ill.

The same officer showed me around the city. He pointed out a pedestrian bridge and said that if we'd been there a week earlier, we would have seen the bodies of three men hanging from it. He showed me a row of buildings with a gap in the middle.

'That was where their air force headquarters stood until it was hit by some precision bombing by Israel,' he said.

I wanted to travel to Beirut with our photographer, Jim, if he was well enough. I told my army friend that I had been promised two armed guards for the trip for a price of $500.

'First sign of a gun, a checkpoint, anything, and they're off,' he said. So we didn't bother.

A few days into the trip, we were running out of money. So I asked *The Star* to wire some out. I went to the bank who denied all knowledge of the $1,000 until I pointed out a Bank of Ireland fax I could see from where I was standing on the customer side of the counter.

The teller said he would give me the money in Syrian pounds, about a zillion of them. I said I wanted dollars. He said no. I asked to see the bank manager and was brought to an office to see him. He said no. I went to the Central Bank and saw someone in a big office who kind of said yes and no at the same time. He said, maybe I'd get half and half.

So I asked my Army friend to help. He said he'd come with me. We went back to the bank where this saga had begun. The same clerk was behind the counter. The Army Officer whispered in my ear.

'If you really want him to be helpful, tell him his father must have been a wonderful man to produce a son like him.'

I reacted instinctively. 'Fuck off. You're taking the piss. Is there a candid camera on me or what?'

He was serious. So I said it. Out loud.

'Your father must have been a wonderful man to produce a son like you.'

He beamed with pride. He looked around to make sure everyone had heard me and he smiled. Then he offered to give me the money, half in Syrian pounds and half in dollars. It worked!

Different culture. I had to be taught. Oh. And Brian Keenan didn't get out that time.

The People One Meets (Part 1)

John Wayne

There is almost an industry in reminiscing about John Wayne and his links with Ireland. And it's all because it is now more than 60 years since *The Quiet Man* was filmed in the West of Ireland. For me, though, it is a summer's day in 1974 in Dublin that I will forever mark as my John Wayne Day.

I wasn't long working in the *Evening Herald*. I was the cubbiest of cub reporters. My news editor asked me to stroll up to the Gresham Hotel because someone had called to say John Wayne was there. My job, he said, was to get an interview. Why ask a cub reporter? Well, I suspect largely because in the first instance, they didn't believe John Wayne was there. And even if he was, big movie stars didn't simply give interviews willy nilly, did they? So send the cub. At least it will get him out of the office for a while.

So I strolled up to the Gresham with our photographer, the late Eamon Gilligan. We headed straight to the dining room having been told that John Wayne was having breakfast there. And so he was.

There was no point in pussy footing about. Either he'd talk to us or he wouldn't so I walked over and said:

'Excuse me Mr Wayne. My name is Paddy Murray and I'm with the *Evening Herald* newspaper. I was wondering if I could have a word?'

He looked up and smiled: 'Sit down young fellar,' he said, 'and have breakfast with me.' And I did, as did Eamon.

'So. I guess you're a reporter,' he said. I confirmed that for him.

'And who do you work for?' he asked.

'The *Evening Herald*,' I reminded him.

'And do you like working for them?' he asked me.

I told him I did as it became clear that it was he who was interviewing me. He asked a few more questions before eventually I got to ask him about *Brannigan*, the movie he was making in London. It was a part he chose having turned down the role of Dirty Harry, subsequently taken by Clint Eastwood. Then we chatted about *The Quiet Man* and his memories of making that classic movie in the west. And we talked too of his admiration for Richard Nixon. A fine American, he said. A brilliant President, he said. A man who had done nothing wrong, he said, just weeks as it happens before the disgraced President quit.

And what had him in Dublin I wondered? He had come, he told me, to meet his 'good friend Lord Killanin'.

'Oh,' I said. 'And when are you meeting him?'

'I'm not,' he said. 'He's in Zurich.'

So on we chatted as he tucked into two fried eggs, a half dozen rashers, a few sausages, tea and toast. He was, it has to be said, a thorough gentleman, and he made sure that there was tea and toast for us too. Eamon was a little disappointed that John didn't know Richard Harris, who Eamon did know, but still, we had a nice chat.

As I stood to thank him – deadlines, you know, we could have talked all day otherwise – he asked me where he might get a 'bainín hat and a blackthorn stick'.

There was a souvenir shop just up from the main door of the Gresham back then, where Toddy's bar is now, so John and I – he didn't mind me calling him John – walked up O'Connell Street to the astonishment of the city's citizens. Eamon snapped away with his camera, taking photographs of the movie star and the cub reporter. And while John managed to get his souvenirs, I sadly, have none. I have no idea where that picture is now, though I would happily give my left arm for it.

Even without it though, I still have a pretty unique boast if ever a conversation turns to John Wayne. Did I know him? Of course I did. Sure, we had breakfast together.

Donovan and Dean Friedman

A long time ago, Liam Mackey and I hosted a programme on Today FM called *Murray and Mackey*. It had various elements, a bit of comedy, a two-handed (comedy) soap opera with multiple characters – and an interview.

One week, it was legendary singer Donovan who, at the end, invited Liam and I to join him singing 'There is a Mountain'. We did. Only I more or less stopped singing after a while and mimed. Liam wasn't happy.

Some weeks later, Dean Friedman was our guest. He brought his electric piano and he sang. Then Liam suggested Dean and I sing 'Lucky Star' together, with me taking the female part. I told him, quite smugly, that I couldn't because I didn't know the words.

'We thought of that,' he said.

And he produced a sheet of paper with the words, which I already knew, printed on it. So Dean Friedman and I sang 'Lucky Star' on national radio with me taking the female role. It was Liam punishing me for miming with Donovan.

Madonna

The meeting with Madonna was unusual. I was in New York in the Columbus Bar and Restaurant. A friend, Martin Sheeran, and his wife Mary Pat Kelly had brought us. We were sitting at a table with the Vice President of Paramount Pictures. The other person at the table (he told us when she had gone) was an actress called Helen Shaver 'who was in that lesbo thing', he added, referring to a movie called *Desert Hearts*.

Anyway, also in the restaurant that night were Darryl Hall and John Oates, Simple Minds and a few actors and actresses. We tried to remain calm and not look impressed. Until Madonna and Sean Penn came in.

Well, it was March 16, the night before St Patrick's Day, and I was in New York writing the Social Diary for the *Evening Herald*. And it was Madonna. I had to. But I knew if I approached her, I'd be out on my ear. In fact, if they knew I was a journalist, I'd be out on my ear. So I formulated a plan.

Every time she went down to the loo, I gave it some time and went down hoping to bump into her. I got lucky. I was just at the end of the stairs when she emerged from the ladies.

'Howya?' I said, in the thickest Irish accent I could muster.

'Hi,' she said. 'You over for Patty's Day?'

'I certainly am,' I said, laying it on thick. 'Are you celebratin' yourself?'

'Oh, I'll enjoy it,' she said. Or something like that. It didn't matter.

The diary next day began, 'Bumped into Madonna in New York last night ...'

James Taylor

James Taylor was interesting. I interviewed him in a scruffy little room at the back of the National Stadium, where he was to play that night. I was told that under no circumstances was I to mention (a) Carly Simon (his ex-wife) or (b) drugs. Well, the interview was a bit monosyllabic.

'You have a new album coming out?'

'Yes.'

'Where are you going after Dublin?'

'London.'

And so on. It was embarrassing. So, despite the fact that the PR minder was there I just came out with it.

'Do you see much of Carly these days?'

'Oh yes,' he said and went on and on about her.

And when he'd finished I asked him about drugs, he being a former addict. Again, on and on he went. Great interview. Lovely guy. Sometimes, the PR people issue instructions they think their clients want issued. Reality is often different.

Pele

I met Pele in Temple Street Children's Hospital. He was brought there by a charity to see the children. It was a fairly predictable chat with a man who, at the time, didn't have much English. I asked him if had been educated at any time by the Irish Christian Brothers. He said he had.

'Did you know,' I asked him then, 'that the Irish word for football is *peil*?'

He laughed. He didn't know. And then he said it was as good an explanation as any he had heard for his nickname. I can just hear it how. A Christian brother calling a soccer-mad young fella. 'Oi. Soccer.' Or, just out of habit, 'Oi, Peil.'

Spike Milligan

Spike was coming to Dublin to do a show in the Gaiety, and I was told I had ten minutes with him. We spoke for an hour. We laughed, we cracked jokes. I completely forgot I was doing an interview for the paper. He spoke about his Catholicism. It was unorthodox and I remember writing at the time how he believed that the Church should be bringing truckloads of condoms *into* Africa, rather than banning them. I didn't use that until he had died – I told him I wouldn't. It would have caused him such grief.

Although the world had moved on since John Lennon's misunderstood line about the Beatles being more popular than Jesus, I didn't include in my interview for the *Herald* Spike's fairly explicit remarks about how he thought Jesus Christ would react if he met the Pope. I did include them, as I promised him I would, in his obituary after he died in 2002.

Spike wanted to be Catholic, but just didn't agree with a lot of what the Church was doing and believed Jesus wouldn't have agreed either.

The best part, though, was that when the interview was over and I thanked him, Spike said: 'Don't be thanking me. I forgot it was an interview. It was like chatting to an old friend.'

Now *that* made my day.

Terry Wogan and Brendan Grace

I was over in London with comedian Brendan Grace. I was hired to advise him and to write his script for his appearance on *Wogan*. During the day, we met Terry and chatted and messed around and joked.

At one point, I was in Brendan's dressing room going through his script (Terry didn't have one) and he suddenly jumped up, ran out the door and up the corridor and burst into Terry's dressing room without knocking. Even from down the corridor, I could hear it. He farted loudly.

A cross between amused and bemused. I think that's the only way to describe the look on Terry's face as he emerged from his room.

J.P. Donleavy

I was on the road for the *Sunday Independent*. Every second week, off I went looking for stories around Ireland. This particular week, I was in the midlands with a photographer scouting around, reading the local papers, talking to people, looking for stories.

Someone told us that a rich stranger had moved into a castle near the town. For the life of me I can't remember what it was called. But I do remember knocking on the vast door and an Englishman answered. I told him we were from the *Sunday Independent* and doing stories around the area. I wondered, I said, if he'd like to tell us about the castle.

He was very polite. No, he said. He really would rather I didn't. It wouldn't be appropriate, he said. It being no skin off our nose, we didn't. And I still don't know who he was!

Nearby, though, lived the writer J.P. Donleavy who, we were told, would as likely as not run us if we had the temerity to ask him for an interview. But we drove up, knocked on the door and asked anyway.

He was brilliant. I remember asking him if he wrote all day or, if not, what did he do?

'I like to get up, feed the dogs, and go for a walk on the grounds. Every now and then I poke my walking stick into the earth, as you do, evict a tenant or two and return for lunch.'

He was great value. An author I admired and an interview I loved.

Peter Langan

I'm not a big horse racing fan, but I was invariably sent to cover big horse racing meetings for the 'diary' in the *Evening Herald*. On one such occasion, I was sent to Galway Races. To be honest, I don't like the races. Everyone's too busy, in too much of a hurry, whispering about tips or just plain drunk. Anyway, Galway it was.

And, as ever, I sought out the famous and if I failed to find any famous people I sought out the almost famous and if that didn't work, I sought out people I would make famous, if only for one edition of the *Herald*. And then *bingo*!

I got to meet Peter Langan, legendary co-owner of Langan's Brasserie in London's Mayfair. This was the restaurant he owned with Michael Caine and in which, in late afternoon, he could occasionally be found asleep under a table. Among those who ate there were Elizabeth Taylor, Marlon Brando, Mick Jagger, Francis Bacon, Muhammad Ali, Jack Nicholson and David Hockney. Made for me. And he likes a jar.

So we had a few lunchtime drinks, just he and I, and decided to eat. We went to the, eh, food tent and ate some of whatever it was they put in front of us.

'Dessert might be better,' he slurred. We had wine with the meal too or maybe a meal with the wine.

'Bring us the dessert menu,' he commanded.

The waitress brought it.

Remember, this man ran a restaurant in London, had hired a Michelin starred chef for its kitchen and was about to order dessert.

'I'll have the Black Forest Gateau,' he said, turning to me to add, 'you can't go wrong with Black Forest Gateau.'

'It's not defrosted yet,' the waitress said.

So we went to the bar.

Peter died aged just 47 in 1988. Great company, unassuming – at least, when I was on the lash with him he was. And we had a great day.

Richard Harris

There are myriad stories about Richard Harris, a fine actor and wonderful man. Here are three, two for context and one I can vouch for.

The story goes that while he was living in London with his then partner, he popped out for milk one day and saw in a newspaper that Young Munster were playing in Thomond Park, Limerick that evening. He supposedly got the next available flight to Ireland and spent the next few days on the piss in Limerick. All of this was unknown at the time to his partner, who had no idea where he was. When he finally returned to England he rang the doorbell of his house. She answered the door and before she had a chance to say anything, he said, 'Well, why didn't you pay the fucking ransom?'

The second story involved his departure from Claridges hotel on a stretcher as he was brought to an ambulance and to hospital where he died of Hodgkin's Lymphoma in October 2002. As his stretcher was being wheeled to the ambulance, the story goes that the gravely ill Richard managed to lift his head from the pillow and say to those gathered in the hotel lobby: 'It was the food.'

I can't vouch for either story.

This one I can vouch for. Blackrock were playing in Limerick and, as usual, a large gang from the club made their way down on a chartered train. A few jars were had on the way. A few were had on arrival. A few were had at the game. And we headed for a few more at one of the city's rugby pubs. Well, they're *all* rugby pubs in Limerick. In we went, and who was sitting there having a jar only Richard Harris. Could I leave him in peace? No.

But I had to have something interesting to say. It's important to point out that at this time the Irish rugby team was going through what we always call a 'bad patch'. Things were pretty dire. I knew Richard had once said, when asked about his love for rugby – he was a fine player – that he would give it all up, the fame, the money, everything, for one cap for Ireland. So over I went and introduced myself. I asked him if it was true that he had said he'd give it all up for one cap and he smiled and said, yes, it was true. He had said that.

'Well', I said, 'I think you're closer than ever.'

He threw his head back and laughed and I left it at that. He smiled as we left and looked for another rugby pub. Job done.

Ian Botham

It was 1987. Ian Botham had completed a charity walk from Belfast to Dublin in aid of Leukemia Research. When the walk reached Dublin, Beefy, as he was known, and a few of those who had accompanied him on the walk went for a pint or two – or was it ten? – in O'Brien's of Sussex Terrace.

So I joined them and had a pint with Ian who seemed to be in great form and didn't appear to be knackered after the walk. He said he'd been looking forward to a pint after the long days on the road. I presumed they'd behaved themselves en route. Still, I could tell that PR man Pat Heneghan, a good mate, was absolutely knackered. He had accompanied Ian I think because the walk was sponsored by Harp, a client.

'He's not human,' Pat said as I sipped my pint.

I think Pat himself may have considered joining the Pioneers after the walk. And here's why.

'We'd only just started,' Pat said. 'When Ian said he wanted to go into a shop. A grocery store. So we went in. He went up to the counter – it was the part of the shop where they sold sweets and fags and drink – and asked if they had those two litre bottles of 7 Up? The shop assistant told him they did.

"Well, get me one of them, empty that piss out and fill the bottle with tequila." And she did. And as we walked down the road, Ian would take out his bottle of "7 Up" every now and then and take a swig, And so did I. I am bollixed.'

Legend? No. I'd say it's all true.

Angharad Rees

I can't remember which year it was that I danced with Angharad Rees. If you watched the original *Poldark* series, you will surely remember Angharad. She starred as Demelza and stole the show.

She was in Cork for the film festival and I was working there. I was a guest at the official ball. Angharad was the guest of honour. And without even being fortified with wine, I somehow got the courage to ask her to dance. And she said yes.

The thing about our encounter was that she was charming. She was nothing like I expected a star to be and, at that time certainly, she was a huge star. She was chatty, interesting and interested.

So much so that forty years or more on, I still remember that dance, those few minutes. I almost fell in love, surprised and charmed by how nice she was as well as her beauty. Someone said to me once that maybe she liked me too. I had to remind them what she did for a living. She was an actress! And a wonderful person. Indeed, when I heard she had died in 2012, I shed a tear.

I was invited to her funeral – having told the family of my experience in Cork – but couldn't go because of my health. But I wasn't one bit surprised to read that leading the tributes at the funeral, Julian Fellowes said, 'If there was one thing she was superb at, it was friendship.' I experienced it for five minutes. And remembered.

Kim Wilde

Another beautiful lady. She had just had her big hit with *Kids in America* and was in Dublin either for a gig or promoting a gig. Anyway, there was a press reception in the Deerpark Pub in Clonskeagh. I was dispatched.

It was packed. But I spotted that, for one second, there was nobody talking to Kim. So I went over, introduced myself, and asked if I could have a few words. She said yes and gestured towards a couch where we both sat. We got on well.

After ten or fifteen minutes, some bloke came over and said, 'Kim, we need you now, in the other room.'

She looked at me, and then she looked at him. 'I'm talking to Paddy. I'll be with you when we're finished.'

His face froze. He wasn't used to being spoken to like that.

Kim turned to me and just said, 'Where were we?'

There aren't many in her position who would have had the manners to do what she did. A perfect lady.

Elton John

It was June 1984 and Elton John was playing the RDS in a gig which was 'in association with the *Evening Herald*'. So the editor, Niall Hanley, asked me to go to Belfast two days before his Dublin appearance. It was in the King's Hall and was one of the first major gigs in the city since the 1960s. The Troubles ensured that most big stars stayed away.

It was an extraordinary performance. After the encore, Elton called his band back on to the stage where they performed a medley of Beatles' numbers. A real encore. Outside afterwards, people stood around chatting and drinking pints, car roofs being used to rest pints as people chatted.

And so I wrote a review reflecting not just the enthusiasm of Elton and his band while they performed, but also the fact that afterwards his fans chatted among themselves, no one worrying who was from where or who went to what church.

And so to the RDS. Before the gig, James Morrissey came to me and said Elton wanted to meet me.

'Yeah, right,' I said.

James persisted. I didn't believe him. But he kept saying it. Eventually, I agreed to go with James, warning him that if he was taking the piss I wouldn't be happy. I walked around the back of the stage and was introduced to Elton.

'I just want to say thank you for the best and most intelligent review I have ever received,' he said.

I was stunned. Even better, though, was some years later when Jim Aiken brought me to Paris, along with a couple who had won the trip in an *Evening Herald* competition, to see Elton perform in a sports arena there. He was due to play Dublin again some weeks later. Before the gig, the four of us were brought into the bowels of the stadium to meet Elton. We walked along a corridor, Jim leading the way. Suddenly, Elton emerged from a dressing room. He walked straight past Jim.

'How are you Paddy?' he asked, extending his hand.

'Bloody hell,' said Jim, with a smile. 'I'm paying him hundreds of thousands of pounds to play Dublin and he comes out and says, "How are you Paddy?"'

This, by the way, is the review from Belfast:

Belfast had seen nothing like it for 20 years ... and it's doubtful whether Elton John had either. He did more last night than just perform for thousands in the King's Hall. He brought life back to a city that has suffered more than its fair share of tragedy in recent years. And he performed longer than anywhere else so far on this tour. For 150 minutes Elton and his band belted out the hits, the new songs and even some surprises like 'In the Mood' and a short medley of Beatles' rock and roll songs at the end. The only thing louder than the music was the cheering of the audience between the songs.

He bounced on stage almost on time just 90 minutes after touching down at Aldergrove airport in his private plane, to rapturous applause. As he started the show, wearing pink tails and the familiar boater with a pink band the small were lifted onto the shoulders of the big and the hall became a sea of clapping and waving hands. And when it came to classics like 'Benny and the Jets' he had the audience not only in the palm of his hand but on cloud nine, happier than they had been for years.

To Belfast, he became the Young Barry (McGuigan) of the music world, the man who could make them forget about the divides, the troubles, the violence. He gave them fun, laughter and crack. When he finished and the lights went down, no one was fooled. They just chanted his name – it must have been heard back in Watford until he came out again. He did encores. But they weren't enough. More encores followed. And when he should have turned it down if he wanted the incessant cheering and chanting to end, he gave them 'Saturday Night's Alright for Fighting' and the decibel level rose even higher. He finished as he did in earlier gigs on the tour with 'Song for Guy'. Even that slow instrumental had them clapping. The Dead March would have had them dancing at that stage. And it was over. But the chanting went on 'Elton...' 'Elton...' And back he came.

This time he took his roadies and his band by surprise. The instruments had been put away, but he told them to 'hurry up' and they launched into 'I Saw Her Standing There' and 'Twist and Shout' and then finally with the music still ringing in everyone's ears, it was over. 'I didn't come to Belfast on my last tour and for that I apologise. Anyone who doesn't include Belfast on a tour is a fool,' he said, earning a cheer that almost lifted the roof off and must have made Barry McGuigan think he had a rival.

Outside, he and Belfast promoter Jim Aiken who is also re-sponsible for bringing Elton to Dublin today, could see what good they did for this tragic city. Outside the pubs crowds of teenagers sat on the ground and on the bonnets of cars, enjoying their drinks. They talked about Elton John music and the normal subjects of youngsters. Maybe they did go home in different directions.... This is Belfast. And it hasn't had so much fun in almost a generation, since four young lads from Liverpool filled the same hall 21 years ago. Today it's Dublin. Elton John can do it. He's proved that. Now it's up to Dublin to give him a bigger, better, louder welcome than Belfast. And that will take some doing.

I wrote that in Dublin's *Evening Herald* on June 16, 1984, almost forty years ago. And Elton's still as big as ever, Belfast is more or less at peace, and I'm an old man! Well, oldish.

Dermot Morgan

Twenty-five years ago, Dermot Morgan became Father Ted. But a few short years earlier, well, close enough to another twenty-five years earlier, he had a different name entirely.

It was UCD in 1971. And though Dermot and I both hailed from Mount Merrion and had a nodding acquaintance, we were from different sides of the church. We may as well have been poles apart. But in UCD we became friends and rivals.

I was one of the small bunch who formed a comedy group called The Machine with Brendan Martin and Billy McGrath and, for a while, Brian McCormack and Kevin Kiely. Dermot headed up the rival troupe, Big Gom and the Imbeciles.

Both groups did okay. There were a lot of students and only two groups making them laugh.

Yet another Dermot manifested itself on 'The Live Mike'. He was Father Trendy and though he largely wrote every word the good priest uttered, I was one of the large team of scriptwriters for the show. That ended all of a sudden in 1982 when Mike Murphy declared live on television – and to the dismay not just of the massive TV audience, but to the team working with him – that there would be no new series the following year.

Dermot continued to do stand up and our paths crossed occasionally. He invited me to a late night show in the Oscar Theatre, the former cinema, in Ballsbridge. The largely male and largely half locked audience sat waiting for the show to start. A spotlight shone on the curtain. And then from behind the curtain emerged a girl, stark naked. Her opening line was brilliant:

'May I have your attention please.'

But greater things awaited Dermot. *Scrap Saturday* started in 1989 and changed Irish comedy, certainly broadcast Irish comedy. The brainchild of Dermot and Gerry Stembridge, the show savagely lampooned our politics and personalities. Dermot's 'MARA' character, loosely based on Charlie Haughey's number one advisor, P.J. Mara – the voice sounded nothing like the real thing and wasn't intended to – was ground breaking and massively popular. Our paths crossed again as I wrote for some episodes of the show.

For reasons never fully explained, RTÉ pulled the plug on *Scrap Saturday* in 1991. Dermot hoped to get a topical humorous quiz, *Newshounds*, off the ground, but it never really got past its pilot show. We had linked up again for that, Dermot asking me to be one of the panellists for that pilot which was shot in Ardmore Studios. RTÉ didn't go for it. And then came Father Ted.

You might think Ted was the straight man to the comedic performances of Pauline McLynn, Ardal O'Hanlon and Frank Kelly, but he was no such thing. Dermot played it perfectly.

It wouldn't have worked without him or with anyone else in the role. It was the massive success Dermot always craved, always deserved and finally achieved. He had great plans for the future. He had another comedy show in mind, this time one he was planning to write himself. But he died in London in February 1998.

I happened to be in England on business at the time and so attended the memorial service for a man who had been a neighbour, friend and colleague for so many years. I was asked to report on the service for *The Star* and did so. Several times I wept as I phoned in the story which was how we did it in those days.

The Live Mike was of its day. *Scrap Saturday* is dated of course. But *Father Ted* has stood the test of time. I still watch it and I still laugh as everyone does. Dermot would be pleased.

Jack Charlton

It was February 1993 and I was sent to Albania on a scouting mission. Northern Ireland were playing Albania in a qualifier for the 1994 World Cup in the United States. We were due to play them in the not too distant future so I was on a recce to do a feature telling Irish fans what to expect when they got to Tirana.

The hotel we stayed in was, apparently, one of the best in Tirana. There was electricity most of the time. There was water for showering and flushing toilets for a few hours every day. (When the word came out that the water was on, there was a rush of people to their rooms to wash or go to the jacks.) And almost all the rooms, but not all, had glass in the windows.

The Northern Irish crew had been warned about the food and brought their own and own chefs. We did the right thing. We went on the piss.

And a few hacks, they were mostly soccer writers, suggested we go for a little walk around the city the following morning. I don't think we would have felt comfortable going on our own.

'I'll go with ye lads,' Jack Charlton said. 'Paddy, call me when you're going, and don't mind what I say, just call me and I'll go with you.'

So we drank and went to bed. We got up mid-morning next day and someone asked where Jack was. Bed, came the answer. I was reminded that I had been given the job of waking him. So I went up to his room. The door wasn't locked.

'Jack,' I said.

'Fuck off,' he replied.

'You said to...'

'I said to fuck off.'

'Yes but you told me not to mind what...'

'Just *fuck off*, will you?' And he pulled the covers over his head.

So we strolled around. There wasn't much to see. The only shop that didn't look closed was a bank. We wandered back into the hotel. There was Jack.

'Where were you guys?'

'We went for a walk and...'

'I told you to wake me.'

'Yeh, but you told me to fuck off four times.'

'I told you not to mind what I said.'

Smiles behind his back. Terror on my face.

We got over the not-waking-Jack-up problem and Jack and I sat beside each other at the match. It was a dreadful affair which Northern Ireland won 2-1. Jack made a few disparaging remarks about the game as it wore on. And he clearly was no fan of Billy Bingham. When it ended, he turned to me and said:

'Pure shite. Two shite teams. And if we can't beat that shite, we'll give up.'

Seconds later, as we left the stand, a throng of sports journalists surrounded Jack.

'What did you think of the game Jack?'

'Two strong teams, two good teams, we'll have to work hard to beat them.' Or words to that effect. He looked at me, smiled, and almost winked.

Dr Tony O'Neill

I got to know Dr Tony O'Neill during Italia '90. He was General Secretary of the FAI in those wonderful days. And during the tournament we met a few times for a chat and a drink. I think, because I was reporting on fans and not the players or management, he may have felt more comfortable with me than with soccer writers. Anyway, Italia '90 had to end and it did. And what a time we all had.

It wasn't long after we returned from Italy that Tony called and asked me to meet him for a drink in the Montrose Hotel. I got there and we had a chat about nothing in particular. And then he told me that he was quitting as General Secretary of the FAI. That was a shock. He was telling me, not for publication, but because he just wanted to tell someone. I was dumbfounded. He was loved and admired by the fans. I couldn't understand why he was quitting. I asked him straight out. And this was his reply.

'If I want to get anything done in the FAI not only to I have to convince fifty-six fuckin' eejits in polyester blazers that it's a good idea, I have to convince them it was *their* idea.'

There was no answer to that. So we had another pint.

Eric Clapton

It was 1985 and Bruce Springsteen was headlining at Slane. As ever, working press – and a few others – had access to the Castle and the grounds immediately surrounding it. Great to be able to avoid the crush, but once you got close to the front door, the view wasn't great.

So *Indo* photographer Brian Farrell and myself commandeered a couple of bar stools. And we stood on top, supping our pints, looking at the stage over the heads of the people in the crowd.

'Do you want another pint?' Brian asked.

'Yes. Great,' I said.

'Mind me stool while I go in and get them. Don't let anyone take it.'

'Okay,' I said.

Off he went. And while he was in the bar someone did, indeed, come along and stand on his stool – after, it has be said, asking my permission.

Brian came back. He put the pints on the ground, and before I could say anything he pulled the guy from the stool.

'Get off me fuckin' stool,' he said angrily.

The guy complied and walked away. I shrugged my shoulders.

'I thought I asked you to mind my stool, not let anyone take it?' Brian said as he handed me my pint.

'I didn't think you'd mind Eric Clapton borrowing it for a few minutes.'

Brian looked around. He saw the guy. It *was* Eric Clapton.

'Oh fuck,' he said.

I could see from his face he thought he'd never live it down. He was right. I never let him!

George Harrison

It was 1972. I think. Brendan 'Beamish' Martin was with me. I think. He doesn't think so. Like I say, it was 1972. The brain was in neutral.

Anyway, I went with a friend to the Apple HQ on Saville Row. We went inside and sat down. After a little while, a girl who I presume was the receptionist asked if she could help. I said we were hoping to meet a Beatle.

She laughed and said they didn't come in every day! In fact, they hardly ever did. But she let us stay.

After a long hour or so, I was about to give up when a familiar face approached. It was George. So I stood up and said hello. I told him my name was Paddy and introduced my friend (Brendan or otherwise) and said we were hoping to meet a Beatle and now we had.

He looked somewhat bemused. But he smiled and said hello and we left. Job done.

Gerry Ryan

It was around the time of the thirtieth anniversary of Pope John Paul's visit to Ireland in 1979 that I bumped into Gerry Ryan. He said he was doing something on his show about the visit and asked me if I had any memories of it. So I told him about what happened just before the Pope arrived in Phoenix Park.

We had been told the helicopter would be landing in ten minutes so I decided to go and have a lash. They had set up a kind of swirl of corrugated iron into which male journalists could walk and be hidden from the public while they had a pee. It had no roof. And, as I told Gerry, just as I was finishing I heard a loud noise, looked up and several hundred feet above me was the Pope's helicopter.

'Nice one,' Gerry said laughing.

I tuned in the next morning and Gerry was regaling his listeners with stories about the visit. And then I heard my name. He said that just before the Pope arrived in Phoenix Park, the journalist Paddy Murray had to go to the loo.

'Now the loo didn't have a roof and while Paddy was in there, the Pope's helicopter arrived and hovered directly over it before landing. So the first thing the Pope saw in the Phoenix Park was Paddy Murray having a big shite.'

Bastard. I just hoped my mother wasn't listening.

Ray D'Arcy

I was at a gig in Vicar Street some years ago when Ray D'Arcy was still doing *The Den*, as far as I remember. I was with Connie and two friends, Alan and Linda Murphy. Alan was a colleague on *The Star*. Ray was at the bar and Linda turned to me and asked me if I knew him.

'I'd love to meet him,' she said.

Well, I didn't know Ray, but I went up to him and introduced myself and on the basis of having a column in the newspaper he vaguely knew me. And what ensued went something like this:

'A friend of mine over there would love to meet you and she...'

'Stop,' he said. 'What's her name?'

'Linda,' I said.

'Where does she live?'

'Terenure.'

'Does she have a husband?'

'Alan. He works with me in *The Star*,' I said.

'Kids?'

'Two girls.'

'Leave it with me,' he said.

I left and said nothing when I got back to the company because I had no idea what was going to happen. A few minutes passed and Ray came over.

'Linda!' he said.

She was startled.

'How are you? Is Alan with you? Are you still living in Terenure?'

Linda didn't know what to say.

'How are the girls? Alan still working away in *The Star*?'

She didn't know where to look. But all was revealed and Ray stayed for a little chat and it was just a brilliant moment. Say what you like about Ray. In my eyes, a class act.

Brendan Grace (Again)

I've worked with quite a few comedians over the years. Some were grand. Some were appalling specimens. On stage, making people laugh. Off stage, bitter, nasty, jealous of almost every contemporary, mean, unfunny and cruel.

Brendan Grace was grand to work with. We occasionally shared a pint – though at one point Brendan was delighted when I ordered myself a Spritzer and after asking what was in it, then ordered one for himself because he was on a diet, as I was. Then one day his manager contacted me and asked if Brendan Martin and I would write a show for Brendan which was to run in the Gaiety Theatre for a week. The fee was to be £700. The show was a huge success and ran for three weeks.

So I called into the manager's office on Middle Abbey Street to collect my cheque. He placed it on the desk in front of him. I picked it up. It was for £300. I told Brendan's manager that we could sue for the agreed amount. He laughed and asked if we had a team of lawyers because 'I fucking have. You have ten seconds to take that cheque or you get fuck all...'

I took it. I had no choice. I know there was nothing Brendan could have done about it but I was still disappointed.

Tony O'Reilly (1)

I worked for the *Indo* for many years and so, technically at least, Tony O'Reilly was my boss. I met him a couple of times. The first was at a lunch in Jury's at which he was being honoured. It was, I remember, black tie.

I arrived in jeans and t-shirt not having been told of the formal dress requirements. It didn't bother me that much. I was only there to have a few words with the great man and file for the *Herald*. I was, I think, 20 years of age and so didn't know many people around town, least of all 'famous' people like Tony O'Reilly.

When I arrived, the great and good were sipping their drinks and chatting and I saw Tony O'Reilly talking to someone in the middle of the room. I waited for my chance, standing there, rehearsing nervously what I would say.

'Hello Dr O'Reilly. My name is Paddy Murray, I work with the *Evening Herald*, I wonder if I could have a few words ...?'

'Hello Dr O'Reilly. My name is Paddy Murray, I work with the *Evening Herald*, I wonder if I could have a few words ...?'

'Hello Dr O'Reilly. My name is Paddy Murray, I work with the *Evening Herald*, I wonder if I could have a few words ...?'

I wanted to get it right.

Then the person he had been talking to moved away and I made my move. I walked towards Tony O'Reilly. I took a deep breath to say my line. And he put his hand on my arm and said:

'Hello Paddy, tell me, how are things in the *Herald* these days?'

I stood, mouth open, speechless. Eventually we had a little chat. But it was only afterwards I was told what had likely happened. Tony had asked whoever he'd been talking to who the 'scruffy kid' at the door was. That person probably sent someone to find out and the message was passed back. I was completely flummoxed, disarmed, outfoxed. And taught a very valuable lesson.

Tony O'Reilly (2)

In 2001, a member of my club – then called CYM now called Terenure Sports Club – suffered a horrific injury. Ciaran McCarthy was paralysed from the waist down after suffering an injury during a rugby match. And although the IRFU looks after such players to an extent, some in the club realised it would take a great deal more to look after Ciaran's needs. And so Brian Butler set up a committee to raise funds for Ciaran. More of which later.

I was on that committee and wrote to Tony O'Reilly to ask him if he would make a contribution. He, of course, did and he called me to say that he was going to do so. During the call, we talked rugby and about how the game had changed.

'Paddy, when you and I played rugby,' he said and, after a short pause, added 'but obviously not together...' (well, the age gap was 18 years) and we chatted on.

A few years later, I was at a barbecue in his son Gavin's home in Dalkey. Emboldened by a few glasses of wine, I sat beside Tony and began the conversation thus:

'Do you remember calling me about the Ciaran McCarthy fund?'

He said he did.

'Well,' I said, 'you almost made me very happy that day.' He looked curious. 'You see, you said, "Paddy, when you and

I played rugby" and then you paused and ruined it by adding "but obviously not together". If you *hadn't* said that, I could have told people you were going around boasting about having played rugby with me.'

He laughed, a real genuine laugh.

Years later, just before I had my Bone Marrow Transplant, I was scouting around looking for tickets for the England–Ireland match at Twickenham when the by then Sir Anthony O'Reilly – having been made aware of my impending transplant – invited me to bring a friend (Brian Butler as it turned out) and join him for lunch in his executive suite at the game. He was a wonderful host.

But at one stage, after the main course, as people were chatting, he turned to me and said: 'Paddy, tell that story.'

My mind went blank. I didn't know what he was talking about. It had been ten years! And then it came to me thank God. I told it. He laughed again and we enjoyed a nice afternoon ... if not the match!

News Wasn't Always Bad

The Bomb Scare

It was at the height of the 'Troubles'. It was a Sunday night and I was on duty. The television was on in the background – RTÉ's live show from the Olympia was on. It was an unusual programme in that trainloads of people came up from rural Ireland to make up the audience. It featured Irish stars and was extremely popular. Well, extremely popular everywhere except in our office.

Someone did notice, however, when an announcement was made that the programme was going off the air due to some unspecified problem. Turned out they'd received a bomb scare. A caller had warned there was a package under one of the seats in the theatre. Once the all clear was given – it took forever – I called the gardaí in Pearse Street to find out what happened. The garda I spoke to told me why it took so long to give the all clear.

'Because,' he said, 'we were told to check under the seats for a suspicious package. And guess what? We found a package under every fuckin' seat.' He paused and then explained: 'Sandwiches.'

Lou Grant

Working in *The Star* was, it has be said, mighty craic as well as hard work. But one guy was determined to make the place look like a proper newsroom. So out he went and bought four wall clocks. He put them up behind the newsdesk and set the times: Moscow, Dublin, New York, Los Angeles or some such. Looked very *Lou Grant*.

Until a few days later when he arrived in and saw the signs under the clocks had been changed: Ballyfermot, Carlow, Mullingar and Gortahork, or something along those lines. Looked a bit more *Riordans* than *Lou Grant*.

Putting the Boot In

Conor MacAnally was one of the great reporters in the *Indo*. And a legend. But a legend partly because when he was with the *Herald* he tried to pull a fast one. He'd been up the mountains late one very wet night covering a murder. So the following week he claimed for Wellington boots on his expenses, stating that he had to get them because the shoes he was wearing weren't suitable for the wet terrain he encountered.

He handed the docket to chief news editor Bill Shine. We were silently cheering him on but were kind of shocked when

Bill appeared to blithely sign the docket, boots and all. Then Bill stood up and very loudly said:

'Conor, the Wellington boots. Where are they? They're company property now.'

Story has it that Conor had to go out and buy Wellington boots, cover them in muck and hand them over. Better, he said, than admitting he made up the stuff about the Wellingtons. Not that anyone ever thought otherwise!

A Mother's Advice

I wasn't long in the newsroom when, one day, I was asked to rewrite a few paragraphs about a fatal road accident. And so I did. I handed the copy to the news editor. And I saw him handing it to the chief news editor, Bill Shine. Bill looked at it and signalled me to come to his desk. He looked at me.

'I'm your mother,' he said.

Now, I knew Bill liked a drink, and sometimes late afternoon he might have a few jars on him, but this was early in the day.

'I beg your pardon, Mr Shine?' I said.

'I'm your mother,' he repeated.

I didn't know what to do or where to look. He spoke again.

'I'm your mother. What happened?' he said waving my story at me.

'Well,' I said, 'a 46-year-old man was killed when his car was in collision with a truck near Bray last night and...'

He held his hand up to stop me. He handed the piece of paper back to me.

'Now go and write it like that.'

And he was right.

Me, the Provo

I worked as a journalist in England briefly having managed to get a job on the *Kent and Sussex Courier* in early 1975. The interview for the job was interesting. It took place in Tunbridge Wells, and it seemed to go very well. A posh Englishman – they all seemed posh to me – had spoken with me in his office for about twenty minutes. He seemed happy, I was happy (having been promised that a flat came with the job though it never did) and then he said he had one more question. He looked me straight in the face and asked:

'Are you in the IRA?'

I was tempted to say that he had rumbled me and, yes, I was an IRA volunteer but I didn't. I wanted the job. And the flat! But since the flat never turned up I left after eight months, the rents in Sussex being prohibitive.

A Proper Phone Service

During my spell on the *Sunday Independent*, I would be sent 'down the country' every second week in search of stories about people, a good idea from our editor Michael 'Mickser' Hand. On several occasions, he suggested going to Donegal, his wife Moya being a native. On one such occasion, Michael gave me a phone number to call on arrival. I think it was a sister or cousin of Moya's.

So when I got there, I went to a phone box to make the call, it being a couple of decades before the invention of the mobile. I picked up the handset and dialed the operator. I obviously don't remember the precise number I wanted, but the conversation went like this:

'I'm looking for Kincasslagh 41 please.'

'She's out. If you're the man from the *Independent*, she said to go to the pub and have a pint and she'll meet you there in half an hour.'

No names, mine or hers, but a succinct message delivered. You don't get that kind of service when you call a mobile...

Joe Dolan

I picked up the *Sunday World* one day back in the 1990s and my colleague Eddie Rowley had an interview with Joe Dolan. Can't claim to be Joe's biggest fan, but I always had an admiration for how he stayed right up there all through the years. Then, as I read through, one paragraph jumped out at me.

Joe had told Eddie that what he loved to do on a Sunday was relax, pick up the *Sunday World* and read Paddy Murray's column. So Eddie arranged for me to go to a Joe Show in the Spa Hotel in Lucan where we met up. We had a great chat. Lovely guy and utterly down to earth. Nice to know I had a reader.

Mickser (1)

Michael Hand was the stuff of legend. He wasn't mad about the formality involved in being an editor. He just wanted to edit. Still, he had to attend annual reviews and all that kind of stuff. At one such annual review of progress of the company's titles, Michael explained he was wooing a wider audience with expanded arts coverage, led by a competition for poets and short story writers. A junior director, keen to impress the chairman, interjected to ask:

'And what sort of people entered?'

Michael responded, 'Mainly poets and short story writers.'

His car was famous too. It was a very large green Toyota which was christened 'The Taj Mahal' by his workmates.

Michael also liked a drink. I think Canadian Club was a favourite. One night after several such drinks he was driving home in the Taj – it was a time when everyone drove with a few drinks on – when he was stopped by a young garda on, I think, Earlsfort Terrace.

'You've been drinking,' the garda said after a brief chat with Michael.

'Ten out of ten Sherlock,' came the reply.

He was, of course, prosecuted. And he did, of course, get it quashed.

Mickser (2)

The Eastbourne air disaster robbed us of four colleagues in 1984. Nine died on that flight and four were men with whom I worked closely. There was a massive crowd at John Feeney's funeral in Bray.

We stood there, in silence, waiting for the hearse to arrive so John could be interred. Mickser stood there, close to the grave, colleagues to the left and right of him. He looked shook. And it wasn't just the tragedy that had him looking unwell. He was suffering from chronic back pain, standing there slightly stooped with a pinched look on his face. Indeed, such was his pain that his face looked grey. But he stood there with the rest of us nonetheless. And then we heard a voice.

'It's hardly worth Mickser's time goin' home,' said the voice of Jim, his twin brother.

How we stifled laughter, I don't know, but I do know John Feeney would have approved.

The Ben Lang

My colleague Tom Cryan, known as Squire, spoke in rhyming slang, largely of his own invention. He might walk out of the loo in the Bachelor Inn and announce that 'the Peggy was Padraig'. He meant the smell was fierce – the Peggy Dell (once a famous singer and pianist) was Padraig Pearse.

He would rush off sometimes to catch the 'So Say' – that was the bus, the So Say All of Us.

His best, though, was when we were chatting about a colleague who had revealed that he was suffering from testicular cancer. Someone joined the company and wondered aloud what we were talking about.

'A China who has the Kerry in the charlady's,' said Tom, baffling everyone.

He never explained. We had to work it out. A China who has the Kerry in the charlady's – a mate (China plate) with cancer (Kerry dancer) in the testicles (charlady's ball!)

A Man of Letters

In the old hot metal days, the splash (lead story) headline in the *Herald* was made up of individual metal letters supplied from the lower case room. On one occasion I remember, the headline was to be SAILORS IN SOS. And so the piece of paper was sent to the lower case room with those words and the instructions that it was to be 300 point, or whatever. A sorry looking printer arrived up with the paper in his hand.

'We can't use that headline,' he told the editor Niall Hanley.

Niall couldn't figure out why. It wasn't incorrect, it wasn't legally dodgy.

'Why?' he asked, bemused.

'We only have three S's!'

A solution was found. An S was printed and made into metal and added to the other three. Ah, old technology, you'd miss it sometimes.

Rocket to the Moon

It must have been after lunch. Some story broke down the country and Bill Shine asked Frank Byrne to travel to cover it. Frank said no. For whatever reason, he couldn't do it. Normally, we'd all jump at the chance to put up a bit of mileage so the reason was probably genuine. Bill wasn't pleased.

'Frank,' he said loudly, 'someday they'll be sending journalists to the moon on a rocket.'

And then he added the ultimate threat.

'… and you won't be on it.'

A Good Day for All

Back in August 1986, DUP deputy leader Peter Robinson led an 'invasion' of Clontibret in County Monaghan. Essentially, a couple of hundred loyalists stormed into the town, vandalised some buildings and were run out by the gardaí.

The following August, Robinson and a few of his thugs appeared at Dundalk Court charged in relation to their actions the previous year. I was there to cover it. Ian Paisley was there and got to rant and rave about the Republic.

The loyalists who drove down to support Robinson had their cars stoned as they drove home.

Sinn Féin supporters ran riot and clashed with gardaí. They threw petrol bombs and the gardaí beat the shite out of a few of them. And Robinson was fined – a fine he had to pay or lose his seat in Westminster.

Now back in Dublin, Peter Carvosso was in the editor's chair that day. He heard the radio reports and was getting ready to do a big story about the riots in Dundalk. Until… until he read the first line of the story I filed. It was this:

'Everyone got what they wanted in Dundalk today…'

Because that's what happened. Robinson and Paisley got to complain about justice in the Republic. The Loyalists got to complain about the nasty southern Irish who stoned their cars. The Shinners got to throw petrol bombs at the gardaí. And the gardaí got to slap a few of the trouble makers with batons. A good day for all!

Keith Wood, Jeremy Guscott and John Pullin

As mentioned earlier, Ciaran McCarthy, a member of my sports club in Terenure, suffered spinal injuries in a match in 2001. He was left paralysed from the waist down. A friend and fellow member of the club, Brian Butler, set up a committee to raise funds to help Ciaran adjust to his new life.

He invited me to join, knowing full well I'd be a pain in the arse and argue with him, which I was and I did. But we never let that get in the way of business!

A few fund raisers were organised. But then Brian decided that we'd have a dinner in the Burlington Hotel the night before Ireland played England at Lansdowne Road in 2003. It was ambitious.

CYM was a junior rugby club, and yet we intended to fill the Burlington or at least try. I knew a good friend of mine, the late David Marren, was pally with Keith Wood. I asked if there was any chance he might get Keith to agree to come on the night. Dave said he'd ask, and came back with the news that not only would Keith do it, but former English rugby star and now commentator Jeremy Guscott would join him.

Then we came up with the mad idea of inviting the entire 1985 Triple Crown winning team to the dinner! Astonishingly, all but two made it – and the two who didn't had genuine reasons for not being there!

And then it was decided to ask John Pullin, the famous English captain who brought his team to Dublin the year after the Welsh and Scots had refused to travel due to the Northern Troubles. He had said, after Ireland beat his team, 'We're not much good but at least we turned up.'

And the dinner? It was the biggest *ever* held in the Burlington with 1,222 people in attendance. Well known and important people paid €100 a head to sit elbow to elbow in the packed dining room.

Goldman Sachs chairman Peter Sutherland was invited to speak but declined because he was due at a conference abroad. But when that was cancelled, he didn't just buy a ticket for the dinner, he bought a table.

Roy Keane wasn't there but he had read about it and sent two tickets for Old Trafford and an invitation to the Players' Lounge which was, among many other items, raffled on the night. It raised €5,500 – and true to his word Roy looked after the guy who bought it when he and his family went to the match in Old Trafford.

All in all, the committee raised more than €300,000 for Ciaran. No other club, junior or senior, had ever done anything like it. Nothing makes up for the injury Ciaran suffered. But at least the funds helped him adjust his life.

Some Stories That Mattered

The Stardust Fire

It probably wasn't that unusual, but on Friday, February 13th, 1981, it seemed that half the staff of the *Evening Herald* was giving it a lash somewhere or other, Valentine's Day being 24 hours later no doubt the excuse.

I hit the bed about two or three having spent the evening in the home of a colleague, Peter Carvosso. I was only in bed when the phone rang. There had been a fire in a nightclub in Artane and there were many victims. So I hit the office.

Everyone looked bleary. One man, Michael Brophy, dunked himself in a cold bath on arrival at Independent House before doing an extraordinary day's work! We all did. We had to.

Forty-eight young Dubliners died in the fire. Many more were hurt. I had learned early on in journalism that, when there is a major story, the first thing you hear is generally the accurate one. I therefore believed that the exits of the nightclub were barred and/or chained that night, which was subsequently confirmed.

The work in the office was traumatic enough. But then, as names emerged, some of us were sent out to talk to the families. I was given three names and addresses. And whatever people may think, it is a job which must be done. On jobs like that, I always first called to a neighbour and asked them to introduce me to the bereaved family. Without exception, I was always invited in. I was never treated with anything but courtesy.

I visited two families and got details of the young person who had died and, of course, a photograph. But I couldn't face the third. I was in bits after spending the morning with the two families, both grieving for a young son or daughter. And so, remarkably, the taxi driver went to the door of the last family, having gone to the neighbour first. He emerged with all the victim's details and a photograph. He told me he had explained my difficulty and they understood. Astonishing.

A couple of days later, I was on funeral duty. I can't remember how many I covered. I know that one morning I was in a taxi on my way to a funeral on Dublin's Northside when we stopped at traffic lights and two funerals passed in front of us going in opposite directions.

At the funeral of the two Keegan girls, I finally lost it and began to weep. And in this wonderful, mad city of ours, some friends of the girls comforted me. I explained that I was only a reporter from the *Herald*, but a woman put her hand on my arm and told me 'it can't be easy for you either'. Me, the hack covering the story.

She knew that I wasn't family and had no connection with the tragedy. But she knew that like them I was grieving.

The Hard Calls

I walked into the *Evening Herald* office one morning in the mid-1970s, just before 8.00 am. 'Keep your coat on.' You never wanted to hear the news editor, Padraig Beirne, say those words.

I was sent with a photographer to a tough inner city block of flats where a teenager had been stabbed to death the previous night. My instructions were to talk to the family. I wasn't looking forward to it. The morning newspapers said he had died in a gang attack.

We got there and, as ever, the photographer made some excuse about putting cameras together or some such and told me to go up to the flat. I was trembling as I knocked on the door. It opened and I identified myself. I didn't know what was coming next, a punch, being shoved down the steps – I had a pretty prejudiced view of these unfortunate people. But what happened amazed me.

'Thank God you've come,' said a man, unshaved and red-eyed who was the young man's father. 'My son was in no gang,' he said.

I went in, and since I hadn't been thrown off the balcony the photographer soon followed. They were lovely people, smeared in the morning papers and anxious to put things right. I had deadlines, but also a duty. So I stayed an hour as they told me about the lad who seemed to be not just innocent, but a lovely young man. Knocking on the door of the bereaved is not always a bad thing.

Miami Guns

Guns and America. It's a kind of love affair. So when I was sent on assignment to the States back in the mid-1980s, I thought I'd have a closer look at what seemed to be America's obsession with guns.

I was traipsing around Florida doing this and that with our photographer. Mainly, we were interviewing Irish Americans and putting together stories with an Irish twist. But I kept thinking about guns and why so many Americans owned them. Eventually I linked up with an Irish American cop in Miami. He was just Irish enough to agree to a request from his boss to help me.

We did a tour of the city. He showed me where so and so had been shot and where Officer something or other had taken out a 'perp' and various other locations which were marked, in his memory, by the sound of gunfire.

I asked him how easy it would be for me to buy a gun. So he suggested we find out.

He took me to a Tamiami Gun Store and had a quiet word with the owner, someone he clearly knew. I was to pretend to buy a gun and the shop owner was willing to play along. The cop told me to pick up a rifle and some ammunition and bring it to the counter. So I did. The cost of the rifle and a couple of boxes of ammunition was around $200.

'Here,' said the gun store keeper, pushing an official look-ing form towards me, 'read this and sign it.'

It was a document testifying that I had no criminal con-victions, was an American citizen, did not suffer from mental health difficulties and so on. I signed it.

'What if I'm lying?' I asked the gun store owner.

'Then you're in trouble, not me,' he said. And he invited me to pay him and take the gun and ammunition with me.

'Now,' said my new policeman friend, 'pick a handgun and some ammo for yourself.'

So I picked up a handgun and ammunition and went through the same routine. I put them on the counter. He told me the cost. He handed me the form which I duly signed.

'Come back tomorrow and I'll give you your gun and your ammo,' said the gun store keeper.

I didn't understand. 'Why can't I take it with me now?' I asked.

There was a 24 hour cooling off period, the cop explained. 'Too many Marias killing too many Josés.'

The authorities in Florida apparently believed that hand-guns were used in the majority of domestic gun crime. Hence the cooling off period for handguns but not for rifles. Well, I'm sure it made sense to them.

JJ 45½

There is one grave in Glasnevin Cemetery which I know but hardly anyone else does. It is grave JJ 45½. And this is its story.

Back in the late 1970s I was working for the *Evening Herald*. Then, as now, some people were down on their luck, living on the streets, and I wondered ... do we still have paupers' funerals? Is anyone ever buried whose identity is unknown?

So I asked what was then Dublin Corporation. They said that, on the rare occasions when someone unknown was found dead in Dublin, Fanagans undertakers looked after them.

So I called Fanagans. Yes, they did such work, I was told. But no, there hadn't been an unknown burial for some time. And then, two weeks later, they called back. An old woman had been found dead in a coal bunker on or near Merrion Square. Other unfortunates who lived rough were brought to the City Morgue to see if they could identify her. None could. They tried hostels, charities, public services, but nobody knew her. She was in her seventies, they reckoned. She lived in a city of a million people, but nobody knew her.

Fanagans gave me details of her funeral. It was in Glasnevin and she was to be buried in what used to be the paupers' plot but was now used, I was told, to bury stillborn children. The funeral party consisted of a garda sergeant, the managing director of Fanagans (it wasn't a stunt – he always attended as a mark of respect to the unfortunate deceased), the gravediggers, a staff member from Glasnevin and a priest. And me.

The priest said prayers. We all responded and she was buried. What name would be put on the grave, I asked.

'JJ 45½,' I was told.

'Why the half?' I asked.

'Because,' the sad answer came, 'that's the next number on the schedule...'

A postscript: The editor of the *Herald* at the time wasn't mad about the story. He buried it on an inside page on a Saturday. I heard later that it was read verbatim from nine or ten pulpits the following day. And money was sent to the *Herald* to help the homeless.

A second postscript: A couple of years ago, we paid a family visit to Glasnevin which is a fascinating place full of stories and history. More in hope than expectation, I asked the archivist there if she could tell me anything about JJ 45½. It took her ten seconds. The date and location of the lady's death was recorded as was the location of her unmarked grave. I paid a visit and said a prayer.

The Whiskey

When Pope John II came to Ireland in September 1979, he paid a flying visit to Sean McDermott Street. So flying, in fact, that one local said he whizzed past faster than any joyrider ever did.

Anyway, it was a big occasion on the street and of course reporters from every newspaper, Irish and foreign, descended on this working class, inner city area to cover the event. I was one of them.

I had been there half an hour or so and all I could see were reporters asking the same questions over and over again. I was at it myself. So I decided to find out if there was anyone from the area *not* there. And I was told that one old lady from the flats was too ill to come out. I asked where she lived and her sons – two tough-looking lads – pointed it out to me. They said that, yes, their mammy was too ill to come out and see the Pope drive past. I asked if I could interview her and they agreed.

They brought me up to meet her and a lovely woman she was. Very upset about not being able to get out to see the Pope, but I think delighted to talk to the *Herald*. I had just about wrapped up when one of the boys asked me if I'd like a drink. I said no, I was working. And he asked me again. I kind of said no. And then he asked me again and I realised it wasn't a multiple choice question. I said I'd have a beer.

'We have whiskey,' he said.

I tried to mutter something about not drinking whiskey – I didn't – but before I could say a word, he had a half pint glass filled to the brim. I sipped. I can't stand the stuff. And I supped again.

'Thanks lads,' I said putting the whiskey down.

'You haven't finished your whiskey,' one of them said.

'Yeh but...'

'You haven't finished your whiskey,' the other one said.

And so I downed it. All of it. More whiskey in ten seconds than I'd had in my life up to then.

'Thanks lads,' I said heading for the door.

I went down the steps and as soon as I got to the bottom, I swung around under those steps and puked up the lot.

But then I realised that, you know, they were being nice. They were being generous. Who the hell was I to let them pour whiskey for me and then not drink it? I was sick as a pig, but the episode made me realise that it wasn't actually all about me.

Doug

It was August 27, 1975 and I was living in the town of Uckfield in Sussex. I was working for the *Kent and Sussex Courier*. I drank, most nights, in a pub called the Ringle's Cross Hotel. It used to be filled with locals and squaddies from the Welsh Guards, some of whom were stationed in the town. One reason they drank in Ringle's was because they weren't exactly encouraged in some of the other local pubs. Northern working class and Sussex did not appear to be a good mix.

That night, some of my Neanderthal compatriots planted a bomb in a pub in Caterham. Twenty-three civilians and 10 off duty Welsh Guards were injured. Two of the Welsh Guards lost limbs. I didn't feel like going to the pub. I didn't feel like facing the Welsh Guards who had become my friends. But Paula, then my wife, said I had to go. Of all nights, I had to go. I kind of knew it myself so I did.

I must have been seen passing the window of the pub because when I approached Felix Tidey, the landlord, and asked for a pint, I was told there was 'one in for you'. That's the way it was done in Ringle's Cross. You didn't ask someone if they wanted a pint. You got one in for them.

I ordered a second pint and Felix said it again. 'There's another one in for you.'

And it happened a third time. Now, the golden rule was that you weren't told who was getting them 'in for you'. It worked out evenly in the end!

But on this occasion, I asked Felix, I implored him. I insisted. And he relented.

'It's Doug,' he said.

Doug was a Welsh Guard. A big man who I knew. We'd laughed and chatted and done what you do over a few pints with fellow drinkers. I went over to him.

'Doug, why are you getting pints in for me all night?' I asked him.

'I thought you might be feeling a little bit uncomfortable,' he said.

And I thought of the savages who had maimed his colleagues, the idiots who besmirched the name of Ireland, the hypocrites who claimed to be Catholic or Christian but who murdered and maimed. And I thought of my friend Doug and the basic decency he displayed. And I know which made me feel more proud.

Pandora's Box

George W. Bush, aided and abetted by Tony Blair, ordered the invasion of Iraq in 2003. We know now the consequences of their actions. Endless war, endless misery, the creation of ISIS and other terror organisations.

Back then, I was editor of the *Sunday Tribune*. Less than a week after the invasion, I wrote an editorial about it. My managing director didn't like it and said I should also publish a piece which offered a counter opinion. I refused. This is what I wrote:

Sunday, March 26, 2003

PANDORA'S BOX

IT LOOKS increasingly like the opening of Pandora's Box.

The quick war – not that a quick war is any more tasteful than a slow one – promised by Bush and Blair is already a broken promise. And even though much, if not most, of what we are being told in news reports from Iraq is patently untrue, it is clear that already there have been hundreds if not thousands of casualties.

British and American soldiers have died, been wounded or captured. Towns and cities have been all but levelled by constant bombing. Ordinary citizens are living in conditions of extreme hardship without food, water or electricity and the prospect of disease lurks large. The long-suffering Iraqi people are being victimised by both sides. Iraqi troops are killing their own people as they attempt to flee. At least, that's what we're being told.

On top of this carnage and misery, we now have Bush and Blair telling us they will persist with their ugly, brutal war 'no matter how long it takes'. For 'no matter how long it takes' read 'no matter how many are killed or wounded'. So what if it takes months or years?

Will Bush launch an election campaign in a couple of years' time with body bags and broken bodies arriving back in the United States on a daily basis?

Will he achieve his aim of ousting Saddam after a long and costly war, costly in terms of money and lives, and then simply walk away, leaving to the mortally-wounded United Nations the well-nigh impossible task of trying to pick up the pieces?

Or will he eventually lose patience and use the ultimate weapon of mass destruction?

It is hard to predict what this man will do or, more accurately, what he will be told to do by his hawkish advisors, businessmen all of whom have a clear vested interest in the prosecution and outcome of this war. (Already a massive $1.9bn contract for the 'rebuilding' of Iraq has been awarded to the company of which Dick Cheney was CEO prior to his becoming vice president.) Patience is not a word you can associate with George W Bush. He is in the White House only because the US Supreme Court lost patience with the Florida recount. He went to war having lost patience with the UN weapons inspectors, although Saddam had destroyed half his al-Samoud missiles. He has now lost patience with the speed of his troops' advance on Baghdad and ordered more young men and women to the Gulf where they may kill or be killed.

When Bush opened this particular Pandora's box, he destroyed European unity, he destroyed East/West unity, he all but destroyed the United Nations, he critically wounded the world economy, with all that means for ordinary people everywhere, and he provoked the kind of protests worldwide that gave succour to the Iraqi regime.

What else will emerge from this box before this dreadful business is finished?

I am still proud of that editorial, as proud as I am of any other thing I did in journalism.

District Justice James O'Sullivan

You sometimes meet wise people in your life. The wisest man I ever met was my father. If only I had listened to him!

But another very wise man I got to know was District Justice James O'Sullivan. Jim, as I eventually called him, sat on the bench in Kilmainham Court. I was assigned to be court reporter there, four days a week, for a year or more. It was a fascinating experience. All human life, as they say.

It didn't take me long to realise that Jim was, indeed, wise. But he was also compassionate, tough, kind and eager to help. Jim would almost mock men who stood in the dock charged with assaulting their partners, using drink as their excuse.

'Ah, just drink milk if you can't handle alcohol,' he would say.

He knew. Jim was a chronic alcoholic who had his Paulian moment several years before his appointment to the bench. He had never been violent, far from it. Indeed, his 'boast' if that's what it was, was that he once drank Brendan Behan under the table! But he knew that drink wasn't the excuse it was too often trotted out to be.

Jim sometimes remanded young lads who thought they were tough to St Patrick's Institution for the weekend. Most, if not all, came back chastened.

He told me that, soon after he was appointed, he went to watch another district judge in action. This man had been faced with a mother who kept her children off school. The judge admonished her:

'I won't punish you. You've already punished yourself and your children by keeping them from school. That's punishment enough for you all....'

Or words to that effect.

So when Jim was presented with a comparable situation, he trotted out similar words thinking them wise and, to an extent, compassionate.

'I was then confronted in the lobby by a well known thug and criminal,' he told me.

'You're some bollocks,' the criminal said. 'You had to have a go at that woman and you haven't a fuckin' clue. Why did she keep her kids off school? Because her husband is a thug and fuckin' beats them all. She's afraid to let the nippers out of her sight. She's protecting them, ya bastard.'

Jim told me he learned his lesson that day, a lesson taught to a judge by a hardened criminal. But that's Jim. He listens.

Every case is different. And rather than trot out what he thought were wise words, he would ask the right questions. The thing about Jim is, he was humble enough to do that, humble enough to realise he wasn't right all the time. In my experience in his court, though, he was right about 99.9 per cent of the time. And his kindness, his administration of justice as well as the law, did a power of good.

I don't think this story was a set up, but it certainly suited the campaign of the then newly established Garda Representative Association as they fought cuts in garda resources. And it involved Jim O'Sullivan again.

On this occasion, there was a man charged with drunken driving as we then called it. A garda gave evidence of stopping the man's car somewhere in the Rathcoole area of Dublin. He told the judge he formed the view that the man was drunk and planned to bring him to the garda station to be formally charged. Only he couldn't. Judge O'Sullivan asked why not.

Well, the garda said, due to cutbacks, our squad cars are currently manned by only one garda. 'I didn't think it safe to

All of us in the garden with me, just a few months old, on Aileen's knee, Donal and Úna at the back, John kneeling left, Dee on the ground

My grandfather, Ted Cox, who died in WWI

Saintly schoolboy

First Communion

*With my soon-to-be-priest brother
in the early 1960s*

My father (second from right) at an ESB function

With the scouts – I'm third from the left, front row

Willow Park Under 12s – I'm second from right, top row

Seamus Grace, brilliant teacher in Blackrock College

Three places of employment in London, summer of 1972: The Cockney Pride Tavern (above), The Crown and Two Chairmen (left) and De Hems pub (below)

Two pictures of a Serious Young Man

The John Wayne front page

With Muriel Reddy in the Phoenix Park before the Papal visit in 1979

Must be a junket! Noeleen Dowling, Mary Kerrigan,
Michael O'Toole, Muriel Reddy, me and John Boland

*A gang at Eurovision in Dublin in 1981: (l to r) James Morrissey, me,
Katherine Donnelly, John Feeney and Liam Collins*

*With Shay Healy at Dublin Airport
after his Eurovision win*

*Me at the stone, in the hot metal
days in the Indo*

The photo The Star used before Italia '90

Getting ready to take a penalty against Packie Bonner at some charity thing at half time in a match at Lansdowne Road

A Star gathering of some sort

travel with the prisoner in the back of the car without a garda to keep an eye on him,' he said.

So, he told the judge, he radioed in for another car to come to his assistance which duly arrived. Only the driver of this squad car said he couldn't escort the prisoner in the first squad car because it would mean leaving his car unattended in a remote area. So he radioed in and another squad car duly arrived.

So to take one drunken driver back to the station, three squad cars and three gardaí were required: one to drive the first squad car, one to sit with the prisoner in the back of the car for the journey, and one to mind the other two squad cars until another garda, presumably in another car, could come to bring the car back to the station. Which means that *five* gardaí and *three* cars were required to bring *one* drunken driver to the station.

Judge O'Sullivan kept a straight face but you could tell that he was happy to let the garda tell the story and make his point. And I had the pleasure of reporting it!

A Strange Kind of Justice

I was sent to a district court, not my usual haunt in Kilmainham. It was Dun Laoghaire, and I wasn't familiar with either the judge or the surroundings. But I knew the elderly court reporter who worked there virtually all the time. I was late. As far as I remember I was sent at the last minute to fill in for someone who had called in sick.

I asked my colleague if I had missed anything. He slid his notebook over to me. There was one story. It was about Micky Murphy (we'll call him that as I have no recollection of the name).

'Describing the defendant as a thug and a coward, Justice ____ today sentenced Micky Murphy of Sallynoggin to six months imprisonment for an assault on another man. Justice ____ said Murphy was a disgrace and that his behaviour on the night was unforgivable.' And so on.

I copied it, thanked my colleague and sat back. After about an hour of boredom, another case was called. It was Micky Murphy. And he was from Sallynoggin and charged with assault. When the judge had heard the evidence, he described Murphy as a thug and a coward and said he was a disgrace and his behaviour on the night was unforgivable. He sentenced him to six months in prison. I looked at my colleague.

'Ah well, we get on well, me and the judge, and he likes to give me a story for the early edition.'

Pure Evil

I attended the trial of the notorious killers Shaw and Evans for just a couple of days. I was 'back up', but I remember this. Englishmen John Shaw and Geoffrey Evans were captured after killing Mary Duffy in Galway and Elizabeth Plunkett at Brittas Bay. It had been their intention to kill as many women as possible.

I have one outstanding memory from the couple of days I was at the trial, and it is a sickening one. As I sat there in the court, I could see Mary Duffy's sister across from me. I could also see, almost opposite, the two accused men.

On one occasion when I looked at them, one – I think it was Shaw – was looking across, smiling and winking in the direction of a young girl, obviously related to one of the victims, who was sitting in the court. I don't know if she noticed or not, maybe her grief blinded her to it, but I saw it. And apart from being nauseated, I was infuriated.

My instinct was to jump into the dock and punch his lights out. But I reasoned that such an action might earn him sympathy or even get him off. So I left that anger bottled inside where it still resides.

My Brother's Keeper

My brother Donal was Bishop of Limerick. After what I can only describe as a particularly nasty campaign by some journalists, he had to resign. His crime? He had done something 'unforgiveable' according to the Murphy Report into Clerical Child Abuse, which was not to reinvestigate a case which had been investigated and in which all suggestions of impropriety and wrongdoing had been withdrawn.

It was also a case in which he said, long before any Murphy Report, that he should have reinvestigated when the subject of the original allegations was eventually convicted of abuse.

Anyway, this is what I wrote in the *Sunday World*:

You may have read about my brother in recent weeks. He is or was the Bishop of Limerick. If you were to believe what was written and what was said about him since the publication of the Murphy Report into clerical child abuse in the Dublin diocese, you would say he had no choice but to resign.

He knowingly facilitated paedophiles;

He covered up the activities of priests who abused children;

He moved priests around from parish to parish, knowing them to be abusers;

He received complaints about abuse and didn't act upon them;

He participated in a cover up;

He then refused to resign;

He mounted a 'rearguard action' to save his job;

He fled to Rome where he became 'emboldened' and more determined to hold onto his job;

He went into hiding and

He went to Rome to organise a 'cushy number' for himself.

If any one of these allegations were true, he should certainly have resigned not now but a long long time ago. Only none of these allegations is true. Not one. I know this because, unlike many of those who made the allegations, I have actually read the Murphy Report. Yes there was criticism of him – and others – in the report. The criticism is that in hindsight he could, or maybe should, have done better in one particular case, a criticism he freely acknowledged in 2002.

For the past three weeks I, and other members of my family, have watched, listened and read as our brother was wrongly accused of appalling behaviour. Accusations were made by journalists who, in many instances, seem to have simply made up what they said or wrote. In other cases he was attacked by journalists who spat out vitriol and bile at and about my brother, for reasons known only to themselves.

And he was cast aside by members of the clergy who displayed an utter lack of Christianity and a complete disregard for facts, decency, forgiveness, tolerance and compassion. Some even continued to call on Donal to 'do the right thing' when they knew full well that he had already done so and that he was, probably impatiently, waiting for the wheels of Vatican bureaucracy to turn.

All of this was aided and abetted by a commission which watched in complete silence as its report was misinterpreted again and again and again. This is a commission which, on the one hand, believed Fr Thomas Naughton to be a liar and, on the other, quoted him 'verbatim' in claiming my brother agreed that allegations against the priest were made by 'cranks'.

Throughout the past few weeks there has been no mention of the enormous good done by my brother in his ministry over the past almost 50 years. There has been little mention of the fact that on no occasion did he fail to act on allegations of the sexual abuse of children. The very least he did, according to the report, was to refer concerns to the Archdiocese, where the skills and experience needed to deal with the awful cases resided. This was the established procedure at the time.

Certainly, mistakes were made. The diocesan procedures, and perhaps adhering to them were, in retrospect, good examples of such mistakes. But, if you read the report, you would know that, in the five cases in which my brother was told of specific allegations against a priest, he took the correct action and is acknowledged to have done so.

In the other cases, concerns were raised, but no allegations of abuse were made. Indeed he was not actually handling the three cases in which he was the subject of criticism. In the case of Fr Naughton, my brother asked if there was an allegation of abuse and was told there was not. Nevertheless, he had his 'concerns' investigated. And that investigation, by Fr Naughton's Parish Priest, resulted in Donal being told there was no abuse. When it subsequently emerged that Naughton was indeed an abuser, Donal reported the earlier concerns to his superiors.

As long ago as 2002 he acknowledged that he should have reinvestigated these concerns. He didn't. And it is that failure, *not* his handling of the case or any other case, which the Commission deemed to be 'inexcusable'.

A good man has been vilified. A man whose heart is filled with compassion, who has devoted his life to God and to those less fortunate than himself, who has, by his own admission, occasionally failed, has been scapegoated by those who should and do know better.

The lynch mob has had its day and will now, no doubt, hunt for more victims. I am not surprised at politicians bandwagoning and joining the witch-hunt. It is what they do in their constant search for the popular cause. My anger at members of my own profession, for their utter failure to check facts and for publishing stories, which were utterly and patently false, is intense. My fury at the Commission itself for failing to correct misinterpretations of its report is deep. My disappointment at senior members of the Catholic clergy for their hand-wringing is palpable. But more than being angry, I am sad. Desperately sad. Sad to the point of tears. You may read my words and think: 'He would say that, wouldn't he?' But no. I would not defend the indefensible and nor would any other member of my family. If my brother was guilty of protecting paedophiles, I would not be writing this. But I will defend a good man who may not have done precisely the right thing, but certainly did not knowingly do the wrong thing. If you knew him, you would know that.

He has been damned, convicted without a trial and sentenced without appeal. I doubt that those in the written and broadcast media who have thrown wild accusations about, will have the grace to apologise. I doubt those who said he was mounting a rearguard action to save his job, who said he was, last weekend, more determined than ever to save that job, or those who said he wanted a 'cushy number' will retract their hurtful and scurrilous allegations. Sadly, those who defended him have not, in the main, been heard. So I hope you hear this.

Because, at the end of the day, I *am* my brother's keeper.

We received hundreds of emails in response to the piece. All but three supported Donal.

A Lesson Learned

This had nothing to do with journalism, but the lesson it taught me stayed with me throughout my career. It was about courage, which I lacked, and prejudice which I had in abundance.

It was the early 1970s. Millie Martin, mum of my good friend Brendan, was organising a birthday party for her son Dermot who was born with intellectual difficulties and, to make things worse, was deaf. He was, nonetheless, great craic, had his own way of communicating and he and I got on very well. So I was asked to help at the party which was in the St John of Gods facility in Sallynoggin in Dublin.

The place was packed with teenagers, all of whom had some problem or other. Mostly, it seemed as I looked around, they were Down Syndrome kids. I was putting out juice and sandwiches on the tables as the room filled. I looked around and identified a place for myself to sit between two 'normal' people. Then Millie asked me to bring one more plate of sandwiches to a table. I did, and when I looked around 'my seat' was gone. The only other chair in the room was at a table where all the other occupants, seven or eight of them, were Down Syndrome.

I sat down, embarrassed, nervous, worried. A boy spoke up.

'What's your name?'

'Paddy,' I said.

'Have you a girlfriend?' a teenage girl asked.

'Yes,' I said.

'Do you have sex?' another girl asked.

'What? I, I, I...'

'Where are you from?' asked a boy at the end of the table.

'Mount Merrion,' I said.

'Are you a snob then?' another boy asked.

And on it went.

They took the piss out of me relentlessly. And we laughed and laughed and laughed. It was just about the best time I ever had at a party. It was mostly joshing. But as the meal ended and they were getting up to leave, I did ask the girl beside me what the worst thing was about being Down Syndrome.

'It's everyone saying "at least they're happy all the time" because we're not. We get sad and angry just like everyone else.'

When we all left the table I went to the loo. I locked myself in a cubicle and I cried. I cried out of shame, utter shame that I had not wanted to sit with those wonderful kids, those wonderful teenagers who taught me a lesson. And I realised that if there was anyone in that room with a problem it was me. At least, until they solved it for me.

Michael and the Aftershave

We have probably all known people who suffered from drug addiction. Some of those I know eventually, and with help, managed to beat the addiction. Others weren't so lucky. Friends we thought ordinary like us fell victim to the curse of drugs. I still think of those friends who died. But there was a moment with a stranger which will forever bring home to me the tragedy of addiction.

I worked on Baggot Street in the late 1990s. The *Sunday Tribune* offices were over what is now a Tesco supermarket, in what was once Zhivago nightclub! Every morning, before going into the office, I would buy a coffee in the shop across the street. And as I emerged I would habitually put a few bob into the cup of the young man sitting on the ground begging.

One day I got into the office with my coffee when a colleague, Neil, came up to me. He said he noticed me giving money to the guy begging. And I confess that what I thought was coming next was the old cliché, 'he'll only spend it on drugs'. I couldn't have been more wrong.

Neil, it turns out, did voluntary work with the homeless. He suggested to me that, as well as giving this guy money, I should talk to him. So I did. Every day, I'd get down on my hunkers and talk to the guy whose name, he told me, was Michael. We chatted almost every day about something and nothing. Occasionally he would mention football or I'd talk music. We talked about anything at all. Then one day in late November, I bent down to talk to Michael when he asked me a question.

'What aftershave do you use Paddy?'

I smiled in what was probably a very condescending way. 'Why? Do you like it Michael?' I asked him.

'No,' he said. 'I want to get you a bottle for Christmas.'

I smiled. I said I'd see him tomorrow and I walked away. And I walked away because I didn't want Michael to see me crying. Right up to that moment, I could think of Michael as a beggar, an addict and – a word I hate – a junkie. But in that moment he showed me that he was actually a person, a caring, ordinary person. Yes, almost every thought was probably about his next fix or where he might sleep that night or what he could get to eat. But he had taken time to think of me, kindly, for giving him a few coins and stopping to chat with him.

God, I wish addicts had a political lobby, I wish people marched in huge numbers demanding help for them. But we don't. We give out about them. We blame them for what they've become, though no child ever stood up in class and told their teacher they wanted to be an addict when they grew up.

I never got the aftershave of course. I didn't need to. I got the thought of it. And that thought was one of the best Christmas presents I ever got.

I was told that Michael had died. And more addicts will die between now and next Christmas. We know that homelessness is our shame. But so is the way we ignore the problem of addiction. It took Michael ten seconds to ask me about the aftershave. Twenty years on, I can still hear him asking...

The Mac Stíofáin Hunger Strike

I wouldn't describe my family household as nationalist or republican, but both my mother and father were very proud to be Irish and very proud of Ireland. If there was any resentment towards England, it came from my mother who I think never forgave them for the fact that her father was conscripted in World War I and died when she was just five. But as the seventies dawned I, like many, felt an anger at Britain and at the Unionists in Northern Ireland. And that erupted, for me, on Bloody Sunday.

I was, at the time, a member of the Republican Club in UCD – the 'Stickies' – Official Sinn Féin. And, with thousands of others, we marched to Merrion Square to protest at the British Embassy over the killings. I'm pretty sure there was a petrol bomb or two in our possession. But as time passed, I discovered that they had no real solutions. They had gripes, slogans, plans for action, but no solutions. So I drifted away. And as the violence got worse, it sickened me more and more.

The following year, the IRA leader Seán Mac Stíofáin undertook a hunger strike. I was sent, on one of my first jobs, to a Sinn Féin press conference in their Kevin Street offices. It was my first clash with the Shinners.

A little while into the press conference, I recognised some senior IRA figures there. I asked if they had urged Mac Stíofáin to call off the hunger strike.

'That's not our function,' I was told.

'So why are we here?' I asked.

'Because he asked us to hold a press conference,' I was told.

'While he was asking you, did you take the opportunity to ask him to call it off?' I asked.

'That's not our function,' I was told.

'So why are we here?' I asked.

'Because he asked us to hold a press conference,' I was told.

'While he was asking you, did you take the opportunity to ask him to call it off?' I asked.

End of press conference.

Killing Children

Six years later, after the murder of Lord Mountbatten, his grandson Nicholas, Lady Brabourne and Paul Maxwell and 18 British soldiers at Warrenpoint, Pope John Paul II, on his visit to Ireland, begged terrorists 'on his knees' to give up violence. So some weeks later, at a press conference in Liberty Hall, we faced a load of IRA and Sinn Féin leaders.

Mostly, Americans asked the kind of questions you would expect. The Shinners were asked about the Pope's plea. And they began trotting out a line about the 'Catholic church always allowing a just war'.

I lost my rag. I stood up and walked to the table where seven or eight of them sat facing the room.

'Where exactly,' I asked, 'did the Catholic Church say it was all right to kill two pensioners and two children on their summer holidays?'

I looked at them one by one. They were silent. I looked up and down the line again. They said nothing. So I said:

'Thank you very much for your answer.' And I sat down.

Oh. They showed the clip on American TV. My brother saw it and said, proudly, 'That's my brother.'

A Day in Chains

I was sitting in my office in *The Star* in Terenure in January 1992 when news came through that the IRA had killed eight Protestant workers (for being Protestant) at Teebane in Tyrone. I could take no more.

I drove into Dublin city centre to Parnell Square where the Shinners had their HQ. I didn't know if there would be anyone else there, but it wasn't exactly packed. One man stood on the steps of their building chained to the railings. I asked if I could join him. And I did.

Some Shinners climbed around us. Others went nose to nose (including one young man who, a garda told me, was a bomb designer for the IRA). We achieved nothing, probably, except for a feeling that we had done something instead of doing nothing. My contempt for them remains.

The Golden Days

We didn't realise it, but those of us lucky enough to work in the Dublin newspaper 'scene' (for want of a better word) in the 1970s, 1980s and 1990s were truly blessed. Back then, it had character and characters. Reporters went out on stories, spoke to people, checked things, worked with and against rivals. Those were the golden days.

I'd arrive into the *Herald* just before eight and Padraic or Ray or Martin would be on the desk. Those words you didn't want to hear – 'keep your coat on' – meant you were going off on what was probably an unpleasant job. A murder, an accident, a fire. But if you got to sit down, well, the day began in earnest.

(I truly hope nobody descended from or related to any of those I mention take offence at what follows. All is written with genuine affection.)

Jimmy Cantwell would arrive in. He wasn't always entirely sober even at 8.00 am. But did that stop him being the best crime reporter of a generation? No. He was even better than that.

All our calls went through the switchboard back then, but Jimmy was allowed to use the white phone, the direct line, on the newsdesk. And he did it to great effect, day after day, getting stories for the paper.

Steve Brennan was larger than life too. A seriously good reporter, a nice guy and oozing the kind of eccentricity that made those days and those people so special. Sometimes, though, he was late. On one occasion, he told the news editor that he had received an unexpected call from the airport from a cousin who had arrived in from the US and had to be collected.

'Fine,' he was told. 'Now, Steve, could you get working on the story about the strike in the airport? There hasn't been a flight in today yet.'

He did the story, in fairness. Mind you, his other excuse for being late would probably be in the top ten anywhere in the world, in any job.

'Sorry I'm late,' he said one morning arriving in at 10.00 am instead of 8.00 am. 'The cat broke its back and I had to take it to the vet.'

Oh, we had them all – great reporters, great colleagues, great friends.

Paul Thomas arrived from Bury. It wasn't long before Charlie Mallon christened him Blaggo. Why? Well, Paul was asked to do the check calls, the round of calls to garda stations to see if there was anything happening. There was. And in his Manchester accent, Paul announced, 'Padrig. There's been a blaggin' in Dun Lageer.' He was trying to tell Padraig that there had been a robbery in Dun Laoghaire.

He also reported from the courts on occasion. And one time, he had asked another reporter to write down the name of the judge involved. It was District Justice Ó hUadhaigh. Paul began delivering his story to the copy taker and then took a deep breath before saying: 'Said Judge Robert O Hugadigadi-gadigadigadig....' The copy taker got the message.

Another legendary colleague was Liam Ryan. The word 'ebullient' springs to mind. Liam's life didn't go well in the end which is a shame, but there's little point in telling you what went wrong. He was a good reporter. Better than good. And he never got the credit for breaking one of *the* biggest stories in recent Irish history.

It was a Saturday and I was on the desk as news editor on the *Evening Herald*. We knew that Malcolm McArthur, wanted for two killings, had been arrested the night before in Dalkey. He had been hunted by the gardaí for the murder of nurse Bridie Gargan in the Phoenix Park and farmer Donal Dunne. I heard Liam on to one of his garda contacts. One way or another, it was going to be the lead story and I was glad Liam was taking copious notes. And then I heard him raise his voice.

'All right now. Can we cut out all the shit and will you tell me what the fuck really happened last night. No more fuckin' bullshit. The story.' And he started writing. 'Ah ha. Ah ha. Ah ha. Thanks. Grand. Good. Talk soon.' Or something like that.

He came over to the newsdesk. There were only minutes to go before deadline.

'McArthur was arrested in Paddy Connolly's place. Paddy Connolly. The Attorney General.'

An extraordinary story. On a Saturday morning. And of course because Liam knew his sources, because he was a great reporter, I knew it was true. It was the start of what Conor Cruise O'Brien memorably described as GUBU (grotesque, unbelievable, bizarre and unprecedented). And Liam broke it. Though there are plenty of others who claim they did.

Con Keneally was another legend. A gentleman, great company, a top class hack. And a man who liked a pint. Con had a nickname, 'Bonkers', though he was anything but. I was fortunate, over the years, to sit in the Oval and have a few pints with him. But there's one particular occasion which sticks out.

We were enjoying a few pints when we were joined by a bus conductor. Remember bus conductors? Some used to come into the Oval between shifts on buses.

He and Con chatted away for a while, sipping their pints in between. They got on really well. And then the conductor said:

'Do you know what I love about Dublin? You can walk into a pub and order a pint and chat away with people and have a bit of fun and you don't even know who you're talkin' to.'

Con looked at him sternly and issued a correction. 'To whom you are speaking.'

The bus conductor looked as if he had been, well, hit by a bus. He stared at Con for a few seconds. Then he looked at the bar. Looked at me. And walked out. Wounded.

Con smiled. 'Well he was wrong, wasn't he? Pint?'

There were many, many more colleagues. And there are stories about each...

Wood Quay

If you look at Wood Quay in Dublin's city centre today it is occupied by the City Council's Civic Offices. And that's a tragedy.

In the late 1970s, the site was excavated by archaeologists
from the National Museum. It was a treasure trove so a
campaign began to save the site, one of the largest ever Viking
sites found anywhere. Sadly, Fine Gael and, indeed, the labour
unions, insisted the Civic Offices go ahead on the site. You
will see today two 'bunkers' at the back and a more modest
building at the front. The original plan was for four bunkers.
Anyway, led by Fr F.X. Martin, the campaign to save the site
was popular. Had there been a vote amongst the population of
Dublin, it would have been saved. A huge march demonstrated
that support.

The site itself was magical. There were intact wattle streets,
the corner posts of houses from 1,000 years ago, pottery and
even rubbish from the time was found. It could have been a
massive tourist attraction, and it should have been saved for
us, the people of Dublin and Ireland.

The vandalism went on. I remember one day, an Australian
tourist asking me what was going on and when I told him he
said:

'You're like all Third World countries, so anxious to get
ahead you care nothing for your past.'

He was right.

I remember one evening we were watching TV coverage
of the occupation of the site by protesters when the camera
focused in on one of the workers shouting abuse at a protester.
The camera panned back and who was the protester who had
provoked the ire of the worker? Yours truly.

'You're sent there to work not to protest,' my news editor
said.

'Eh, I was on my lunchbreak,' I replied.

Anyway, the Corporation, as it was at the time, said the new buildings wouldn't block the view of Christ Church from the river. That was another lie.

So Wood Quay was destroyed. And did we learn a lesson? No. We built a motorway beside the Hill of Tara despite alternative routes being available. Another unsuccessful campaign for me!

Fortuna

Back in the mid-1980s the Independent Newspaper Group, where I worked, launched a scratch card game called Fortuna. The plan was simple. Deliver scratch cards to as many homes in the country as possible, and then print numbers every day in the paper. Scratch them off and if your numbers came up, you won. Obviously, the idea was that people would feel obliged to buy the paper to get the numbers. Only it wasn't that simple.

Some of the other newspapers objected on the basis that, because there was no skill involved, it was a lottery, and if it was a lottery it was illegal. The judge more or less agreed, and he gave the *Indo* a day to come up with a solution.

Now, I had nothing to do with all of this. Others were looking after the project. Indeed, they had lawyers and PR people and advertising people all over the place working on it. It was costing, I was told, a quarter of a million of whatever the currency was then!

None of those involved had a solution. So my boss, Michael Brophy, called me. I reckon it was in desperation. He explained the problem and asked if I had any ideas. Well, actually I do, I told him. Because one came into my mind instantly. I don't think he was hopeful. What was my idea, he asked.

Well, I said, instead of publishing numbers, publish clues to numbers. For example, instead of putting in '11', put 'The number of players on a soccer team'. Instead of '4', put 'The number of sides on a square'. Instead of '50', put 'Half a century'. And so on. He thanked me. I think there was a glimmer of hope in his voice.

They took my idea to court the next day with ideas for clues from 1 to 99. The judge looked at them.

'Brilliant,' he said or words to that effect. 'That's fine, that requires skill – only don't make the questions too hard.' (That last remark by the judge is, apparently, why competitions such as those on the *Late Late Show* are allowed to ask such simple questions.)

So the project was back on track. Oh. I forgot to mention. Someone still had to come up with the clues. So the Deputy Editor, my good friend James Morrissey, was sent to my home so the two of us could come up with the 99 clues required. He rang the front doorbell.

'I don't believe it,' he said.

I had no idea to what he was referring.

'Your house,' he said. 'The name on the gate.'

I had forgotten. The house was called 'Fortuna'.

The MD Joe Hayes rewarded me with a few hundred quid. 'It's all I'm allowed to give you,' he said.

Slaughter in Fairview

It was sometime in the 1970s. Back then, we did job after job from 8.00 am so remembering a date is difficult but I'd guess 1974. On this particular night, I was on the night town shift. It began at 9.00 pm and finished at 4.00 am.

Not long before I was due to wrap up, I put a call in to the gardaí. There had been a shooting. A man was dead. It had only just happened. As far as I remember, it had occurred not far from Fairview, I think, though a little further north. The precise location is lost in the mists of time. Anyway, I decided it best to go there. Too late for the morning paper but it would give the *Herald* a good start.

When I got there, there were one or two gardaí on the street but all the doors of houses surrounding the scene were closed though lights were on in some. The body was still in the car in the driver's seat and the car door was open. It was eerie. The car's engine wasn't running so the only sound was coming from my car.

As I stood there under the weak street lights, looking at the body, the closed curtains and few gardaí, all I could hear was Mick Ronson's guitar masterpiece version of Richard Rogers' 'Slaughter on 10th Avenue'... The album had come out in 1974. I had bought it.

And that night the tune that was playing as I stood there, looking at the grim and frankly scary scene, was the only sound. And I thought how appropriate it was.

The Drinkers Who Become Journalists

It was also back in the seventies when I was sent to a conference, about what I don't know, but it was addressed by a psychologist. I had been told to have a few words with him afterwards, essentially to see if I could get a few words our readers would understand! But I decided to ask a question which was off the agenda. Why, I asked, did so many journalists become alcoholics?

'They don't,' he said.

I laughed. 'I have to disagree,' I said. 'I work in the *Independent* and there is an enormous drinking culture there. Some guys even arrive in drunk in the morning. Many are drunk in the late afternoon. And the whole thing is centred around pubs.'

'I know,' he said. 'But it's not journalists becoming alcoholics, it's alcoholics becoming journalists.'

I looked at him.

'People will go for jobs which facilitate their lifestyle and peccadillos. That's why paedophiles becomes priests, teachers and sports coaches.'

It meant nothing at the time. But it became very clear as the years went by...

We're Watching You

I was visiting Derry but as I crossed over from Donegal I was stopped at a British army checkpoint. It was manned by Welsh Guards and, as it happened, I was only just back from England where I had lived in Uckfield in Sussex – a town where many Welsh Guards were garrisoned. I spoke to a few of the lads who stopped me and they knew some of my drinking buddies in Uckfield. We chatted for maybe two minutes and I went on my way.

That night, I was in a restaurant in Derry with a local photographer who was to work with me over the following days. As we ate we heard a bomb go off not that far away which barely raised an eyebrow. We were just about to leave when he said:

'You were a long time at the checkpoint today.'

I was astonished. 'What?' I asked him.

'You were a long time at the checkpoint. I was asked to find out what you were up to, chatting to the soldiers,' he said.

I told him I had known Welsh Guards during my time in England. Simple as that.

'I'll pass it on. I don't think it's a problem. But be careful.'

How a Hangover Cost Me

I don't think I ever missed a day due to a hangover. Apart from July 21, 1976.

That was the day Christopher Ewart-Biggs, British ambassador to Ireland, was killed by an IRA bomb near his residence in Sandyford, south of Dublin city. I was in bed when the phone rang at about 8.30. It was my Chief News Editor Bill Shine.

'Are you supposed to be in here?' he barked at me.

I apologised. He told me about the British ambassador being killed and I told him I could be in Sandyford in 20 minutes.

'Don't go to Sandyford,' he said. 'I want you to go to a hearing at the Land Commission on Merrion Street.'

I went. Six hours of irrelevant bullshit. My punishment.

The Secret Talks

I was a union officer for a few years in the *Indo*. Deputy Father of the Chapel. Yes, journalists are a bit too precious to have 'branches' and 'branch secretaries'. Anyway, it was during difficult times at the end of the 1970s and the start of the 1980s. There wasn't much money about so our negotiations were tough. We got one per cent here and two per cent there. But first, we got a nine day fortnight, and then a four day week.

It was intense at the meetings with management. But things were made a little easier by the fact that the personnel manager, Joe McGrane, and I would occasionally share a pint or two after the meetings – at a location nowhere near Abbey Street – and talk a few things through. Very few people knew. Until now.

A Moment I'm Not Proud of

It's not something I boast about, but if you look at the old In-dependent House on Abbey Street you'll see, jutting out from the second floor, the building's clock. There's a little platform leading out to it. And I wasn't the only reporter to stand on that platform with ... Jimmy Saville!

He took part or even led the annual *Evening Herald*/Central Remedial Clinic walk from the city to Baldoyle Racecourse. He presented *Top of the Pops* and to us younger reporters he was an icon. Now, we know, the emphasis is on 'con'.

No Daddy for Christmas

It sounds cruel, and it was. Let me say that journalists don't always barge in where they're not wanted. Most actually have a conscience. Most have standards. Most have feelings.

It was, I'd say, late 1970s. A few days before Christmas. I went into the *Herald* and was given that instruction we all hated at 8.00 am – 'Keep your coat on.'

There had been a road accident the previous night. Two men were killed. They were married to sisters and because one family was between houses, the two families were sharing a house, temporarily, in a north Dublin housing estate. Two sisters, now widows, with three or four young children between them.

'Go and do me a No-Daddy-for-Christmas Story.'

I went out. But I did what I always did in such cases. I went to a neighbour to ask advice. I knocked on the door, introduced myself, and asked if they thought it would be okay for me to call to the house.

'Oh God no,' the lady of the house said. 'We had the young garda here who had to break the news to them. He was in bits. Crying his eyes out. The priest was the same. And even the doctor looked shattered when he left them. Oh God, don't go near them.'

So I didn't. I went back to the office and told them I hadn't knocked. I had been told that the two ladies were in no fit state to talk to a newspaper. It didn't go down well. Sometimes, newspapers go too far. Sometimes, you have to say no.

The Hillsborough Final

There is probably not a sports fan alive who doesn't know where they were when the news broke about the Hillsborough disaster. Ninety-six people, ninety-six sports fans, crushed to death. It was hard to take in.

I was sent to the cup final that year, 1989. As it turned out, it was a Merseyside Derby as Liverpool and Everton lined up at Wembley on May 20. I travelled with photographer Noel Gavin from *The Star*. I had two tickets, one each, but as it turned out Noel already had a photographer's pass. So when we got to Wembley, I decided that, as the spare ticket cost us nothing, we'd give it to a fan we thought deserving, if we could find one. I thought approaching a bobby was the best plan. So I went to a policeman and told him the story. Spare ticket. Cost nothing. Free to a 'deserving' fan.

'I have the man for you,' he said. 'I almost arrested him a couple of minutes ago for threatening someone.'

That didn't sound like the 'deserving' fan I was hoping for, but then he explained:

'This guy was looking for tickets and listening to the touts and the prices they were asking,' the policeman said. 'Then he heard this tout who was charging way over the odds. Problem was, the tout was a Scouser and this guy thought it bad taste, out of order, for a Scouser to be scalping people, in the circumstances. There he is.'

And so the guy sickened by the Scouse scalper got the ticket. Fair dues to the bobby.

Becoming an Editor

And so it came to pass... I joined the *Tribune* in 1999. Matt Cooper asked me to become his Deputy Editor. Now, I never found out if he was actually prompted to do so by the *Independent*. I presume so. It certainly suited them to move me from the *Star* where, to put it mildly, I was having a bit of a problem with the Editor, Gerry O'Regan, or more likely he was having a problem with me. No idea why. I tried really hard but...

I wasn't actually in the *Tribune* that long when I was offered the job as Managing Editor of the *Sunday World*. Sadly, one of my failings is loyalty, so I declined having only recently accepted the *Tribune* job from Matt.

Then, a couple of years later, Matt was offered the full time job in Today FM. He was no longer that happy in the *Trib*, I think, so off he went. I was Acting Editor and then Editor for about three years. It wasn't easy.

It should have been wonderful. I spent my life working with great journalists, but the team in the *Tribune* was just unbelievable. It was, in my mind, the finest bunch of journalists in the country.

The problem was that the *Indo* had little or no interest in the *Tribune*. It was seen as simply a means of blocking the growth of the *Sunday Times*. So there was no investment in marketing the *Tribune*. Had it been marketed it could easily have become the biggest Sunday newspaper. Matt had built up an extraordinary team and I had added to it as well. But there was no support. Indeed, I'm convinced that if we had managed to creep up on *The Sunday Independent* as well as the *Sunday Times* the plug would have been pulled long before it was.

Jim Farrelly, who was first Managing Director and then Managing Editor, was a nice guy. But his ideas and mine didn't always gel. I did some good things. We introduced, at my suggestion, classical music CD giveaways. Worked fantastically. So much so that several other newspapers copied us. And then Jim took charge of it.

We added the magazine *I* to the package. Jim didn't like the name, but I did and I insisted.

Jim wasn't sure Lise Hand was the right person to edit it. She certainly was. She edited it brilliantly. It was the best of its kind. Innovative, informative and entertaining.

And it was all going in the right direction – apart from some profligate spending in areas other than editorial – when I got sick and ended up in hospital with my damned lymphoma.

Then Jim was fired. Lots of people told me I was safe because they thought I was, including the chairman Gordon Colleary who I admired and with whom I had an excellent releationship. But I got no call from the new MD, Michael Roche. So I called him.

He suggested we meet and asked if I could get out of the hospital for a few hours. So we met in a pub. Ten minutes in, this:

'How would you feel if you weren't editor?' And then: 'I want someone who's there all the time, not someone who's sick.'

Fired. A week or so later he called to tell me he was putting in the notice of the appointment of the new editor. I was with others and some instinct told me to put it on speaker phone. And he said this:

'I'm going to add a line saying that you want to take on a less onerous role.'

I told him he couldn't do that. 'I'm not that effin' sick.'

'You are sick,' he replied. 'You have cancer. Let's use it to our advantage.'

I laughed, I really did, though I suppose Michael was trying to be helpful by making it appear that I had quit on health grounds rather than being sacked. But it still sounded very odd to me.

After it all though we had a couple of pints together in Terenure Rugby Club a few years later...

My Broadcasting Career
(What's the Opposite of Glittering?)

The Talent Show Experience (1)

Back in the late 1970s or early 1980s, I was asked to be one of the judges on a talent show which was being held in a place called The Embankment in Tallaght. It is long closed.

There were many talented acts. And I, along with a colleague called George Plunkett who was also a professional singer in his spare time, and someone else I can't remember, were asked by Joan Byrne to form the judging panel. George was the only local on the panel.

So we watched the acts and went in behind the stage to make our decision. We voted. And the winner was almost unanimous, a band from Northern Ireland called Ghost of an American Airman. They were brilliant.

'That was easy,' I said.

'No,' George said with a look of panic on his face. 'We can't.'

'Can't what?' I asked.

'Can't give it to them.'

'Why not?'

'They're not from Tallaght.'

It seems that it would be unwise for us to give the first prize to an outsider and, indeed, the other acts were by and large local. We discussed it. Joan didn't ask us to change it and we didn't. Ghost of an American Airman it was.

And so the MC went out and announced third prize. It was a local. Big cheer. And he announced second prize. A local. Big cheer. And then he announced the winner. Ghost of an American Airman. Silence.

We didn't exactly sneak out of the place, but we didn't hang around for a pint either. I walked quite quickly to Joan's car for her to get me home. Thought it best.

The Talent Show Experience (2)

Back in the 1980s, I was invited to sit on the judging panel for an RTÉ show called *Screen Test*. I can't remember how often I did it, but I do remember one episode in particular.

I was encouraged a little bit to be the unpleasant one. We watched the acts and were to give each a mark from one to ten. We had cards in front of us with the numbers on them.

A family band appeared, fronted by a girl of about 11 with her uncles playing the instruments. They weren't too good. So I gave them one, commenting that the girl should be at home in bed. I should have known better. As I was walking down the stairs in RTÉ on my way out, her uncles were walking up. One of them stopped me, put his face close to mine and spat the words:

'She's only a child, ya bollocks.'

And do you know what? He was right.

The Talent Show Experience (3)

Well, not a talent show so much as Eurosong. I was asked to sit on the (ahem) expert jury for Ireland's National Song Contest in 1987. It was held in the Gaiety Theatre in Dublin. Most of the songs were forgettable. But Johnny Logan was back for another bite at the cherry. He sang 'Hold Me Now' and I was proud to hold up my card and give him 10. He won. And he won Eurovision. See? It's not all bad.

Then again, maybe that wasn't a disaster because I didn't have to open my mouth much.

The Lyrics Bored

Aonghus McAnally used to host an RTÉ game show called *The Lyrics Board*. The premise was simple. Each team had a piano and a team captain who was joined by two celebrities or singers (!) on either side. A team would choose a number from one to five from 'the board', revealing a word. The team would then have to sing a song with that related word to remain in charge of 'the board'. So far, so good.

Sadly, I think the song we got was 'Agadoo'. Not a single clue did I have. We had to sing along, and I was caught on camera trying to mime. Badly. My lips were not making the words which were being sung by my teammates. It was so bad that some people involved allegedly wanted the episode canned. It wasn't. Sadly, it was aired. I didn't watch.

Line Dancing and Me

Again in the 1980s, RTÉ had a line dancing competition. Brian Carthy was a judge and so was I. I have no idea why. Brian had some idea what he was talking about. I had none. The end.

A Large Embarrassment

Derek Davis called. He asked if I'd like to be in the small audience for his show, *Davis at Large*. They were going to be discussing sport and physical fitness and what different things people were doing. Of course, I prepared well. I'd a feed of drink the night before.

The studio they used, if I remember correctly, was in what was then the Catholic Communications Centre at the top of Booterstown Avenue. Small. And hot. As the lights beamed down on me, I began to sweat and, stupidly wearing a light blue shirt, it began to show. Off camera, I caught Derek's eye and shook my head to indicate I didn't want him to come to me. He seemed to agree and nodded. Dumb move.

Minutes later he addressed me and, as the camera swung around to catch me in full sweat, drips on my forehead, dark blue stains on my shirt, Derek said:

'So, Paddy Murray of the *Evening Herald*, what are you doing to keep fit apart from sweating profusely?'

Can't really blame him.

The Pilot Crashes

In the 1980s (yes, I was busy) Dermot Morgan made a pilot show for RTÉ called *Newshounds* – sort of a *Have I Got News For You* for Ireland. He asked me to take part in the pilot show which was being filmed in Ardmore Studios. The day of recording, I woke up with a smothering cold. I could barely speak. I could hardly think. But out I went. I explained to Dermot that I was stuffed and not feeling great.

'You'll be fine,' he said.

I wasn't. I barely said a word. I sniffed throughout as inaudibly as possible. I stifled coughs for an hour. I was afraid to speak in case I coughed. So I said barely anything. RTÉ didn't buy the series. And I take some of the blame!

The Opposite of a Hit Record

I'll put this in here because, well, it's not really television but arose from my association with Shay Healy through television. Indeed, Billy Magrath and I once did a private show in Shay's house for a party he was hosting. Anyway, Kenny Rogers had a song out called 'Lucille' which was really popular. So I had a go at a parody. I'd been writing parodies for years and kind of fancied myself at doing them. I did most of it and didn't know where to take it until it dawned on me – Shay. So we finished it off between us and Shay released it. The words I remember are:

> In a bar in Marino,
> The mot drinkin' vino,
> And me drinkin' bottles of stout,
> I put me hand up the gúna,
> Of a young wan called Úna,
> And the missus got up to walk out.
> And when I tried to stop her,
> She hit me a whopper,
> With her knee and my eyes filled with tears,
> And when I did wake up,
> I looked through her make up
> And humbly I said words like these.
> You took a fine time to knee me Lucille,
> Right in the guts, you don't know how it feels,
> I know I was wrong now I'm singing this song
> You picked a fine time to knee me Lucille.

Well, it was released and it broke all records for sales in Ireland. Two, I think. And I bought one of them. The only good thing was that because it was a parody my name didn't appear on the credits. It only appeared on the flip side of a song Shay wrote and which was nice in which I wasn't involved at all. And another career bit the dust.

The People One Meets (Part 2)

Spandau Ballet and Def Leppard

I can't remember the date or why I was asked. But I was. I got together a team of journalists to play a team of rock stars in a 'celebrity' five-a-side soccer match in UCD for some charity or other. I don't remember that either. I do remember sitting in the changing rooms beforehand with my good friend and colleague, Tommy Murdiff.

'Rock stars,' we mocked. 'We're playin' feckin' rock stars. Namby pamby rock stars,' we sniggered. What a laugh this was going to be.

The rock stars in question were members of Spandau Ballet and Def Leppard. I know Steve Norman played, in goal I think. The Kemps played I'm almost sure. And Tony Hadley was there but whether he played or not, I don't remember. A couple of Def Leppards turned up too, definitely including Joe Elliot. At the time, Joe and other Leppards lived in Dublin and the Spandau lads had moved to Dublin temporarily to take advantage of the artists' generous tax relief.

Anyway, the game.

Tommy and I probably had a few beers to be honest. I mean, why not? Rock stars! This would be a walk over. And it was. For them.

God they were good. I think the final score was 6-0 or something. In fact, the closest we came to getting a goal was my effort. And I was playing in goal!

I remember Joe Elliot tripping me up when I was on a good run and had tricked the ball past him. But we were humiliated.

111

And of course, the crowd – largely female – was unanimously on the side of the rock stars. We were booed at every turn. Lesson learned.

Charlie Haughey

There were two general elections in Ireland in 1982. The first, in February, was notable because for the first time the candidates were on the pirate radio stations which were springing up all over the place at the time. Charlie Haughey led Fianna Fáil to victory but his government only lasted until November when Tony Gregory and the Workers' Party refused to support budget cuts.

RTÉ had been furious during the previous campaign when candidates appeared on pirate radio stations which were, after all, illegal. Broadcast unions, and broadcasters, indicated that any candidate who appeared on a pirate radio station would not then be allowed on the 'official' airwaves. Suddenly, not a single politician from a recognised party appeared on a pirate station. An edict had been issued. Or had it?

Largely to cause mischief, I went to one of Charlie Haughey's press conferences. And, after a few routine questions had been asked, I put my hand up. P.J. Mara whispered in Mr Haughey's ear. He pointed at me. 'Mr Murray.'

'When,' I asked him, 'did Fianna Fáil change its policy in relation to pirate radio stations resulting in none of the party's candidates appearing on their programmes?'

'There has been no change,' Haughey said, pointing his finger at some other hack.

'Sorry Taoiseach, there clearly has been a change. During the last campaign only a few months ago your candidates appeared regularly on pirate stations. This time they don't. Why not?'

'We've issued no instructions,' he said, again pointing at some other journalist.

'I must insist,' I said. 'There has been a clear change and an instruction has clearly been issued. My question is, when did that happen?'

He didn't like it. He wasn't used to being challenged. He didn't know I was only acting the eejit trying – and succeeding – to rattle him. He stared. I was about to ask him again just to rub it in. And then a colleague, believe it or not, spoke loudly from the back.

'Can we get back to the economy, Taoiseach...?'

And Haughey breathed a sigh of relief.

It wasn't important other than, briefly, seeing the scoundrel begin to squirm. But 'friends' had come to the rescue. Damned shame. Mind you, as soon as the press conference was over, P.J. Mara came over to me.

'You're a terrible bollocks, Murray. Will I see you in Scruffy's for a pint later?'

Barry John

It was 1995 and I was in South Africa for the Rugby World Cup. Our first match saw us stuffed by the All Blacks at Ellis Park in Johannesburg. Good reason for a piss up. Ah sure, any result was a good reason for a piss up. Next morning, I was feeling a bit rough. So I went to the bar. I think it was for a coffee but it might have been for a cure. Next thing, I get a tap on the shoulder.

'Excuse me, you're Paddy Murray aren't you?'

'Eh, yes,' I said, immediately recognising Barry John, the legendary Welsh outhalf.

'Do you mind if I have my picture taken with you?' he said.

113

I thought I was still drunk or asleep or maybe even dead. He stood beside me. And then I saw through the crack in the door the lads from Dundalk RFC who had put Barry John up to it. Bastards!

On Murray and Mackey

Murray and Mackey was our programme on Radio Ireland, later Today FM, which ran for exactly 100 episodes in 1998 and 1999. It was mighty craic. Liam Mackey and I presented and Brendan Cronin produced. It opened with a 'phone message' from some person in the news that week, followed by the theme to the *Rockford Files*. Then we'd chat, play the Worst Record of All Time – boy were there contenders for that title – and followed it with our interview.

We had, among others, Christy Dignam from Aslan who told of how he clung to a bus stop in, I think, Drumcondra one day when the world literally turned upside down (in his mind) due to his drug taking. We had Bertie Ahern on the morning after a British General Election who said, when asked about Michael Portillo losing his seat, 'It was the only time in the whole night I stood up and cheered.'

We had The Beatles, well, The Quarrymen with some of the original members of the group which, in part, went on to be The Beatles.

Peter Sarstedt was delighted we didn't ask him to sing 'Where Do You Go To My Lovely' – there was an awful lot more to him. We had Jason Byrne and, on one notorious occasion, the Aprés Match crew with Ding Dong Denny O'Reilly. Their obscene, but very funny, banter almost got us fired and maybe, in the end, it did!

Ronnie Drew was another guest as was Con Houlihan who held his hand over his mouth throughout so not a word could be understood by the listeners. Brendan Kennelly was charming and funny and interesting. And we had our five minute soap opera set in the post office in Ballyslaphappy.

It was all great fun and had a decent following. Gay Byrne's former producer John Caden had a senior role in the station until it was taken over by Chris Evans' company. John had wanted me and Liam – with Brendan presumably at the controls – to present a two hour show every weekday morning. Indeed, we were told our names and pictures would 'be on the sides of buses'. But we were shown the door instead.

Albert Reynolds

Albert was my favourite Taoiseach, probably because he was the one I knew best. So here are a few things I remember about my interactions with him. We had two general elections in 1982, and for the second I was sent to Longford for the last few days and the count. The instruction was to shadow Albert. Well, there was no shadowing. He welcomed me. The most memorable moment came at the count after the result had been announced and Albert had, as ever, topped the poll.

And old man came up to him and said, 'I did well for you again yesterday Albert.'

Albert looked at him. 'You did not,' he said. 'There were 47 votes for me in your box last time and this time I only got 45!'

The man was taken aback. But then he said: 'Oh. I know. Mrs So-and-so is in hospital and Mr What's His Name is on holidays.'

Albert smiled. 'Fair enough.'

He knew every vote.

I remember too how he solved our telephone crisis. If you remember, back then, it could take more than a year from ordering a phone to getting one installed in your home. Indeed, houses were advertised as being 'with phone line'. Albert told me that on a visit to Cork in his capacity as Minister for Posts and Telegraphs, he called on an office where applications for phone lines were dealt with. He asked the man in charge why it took so long for people to get telephones.

'Well,' the man apparently told him something like this, 'you have to fill in two forms and then those forms are copied here and each one has to be approved by three different departments and when that's done we have to check with the feasibility officer and...'

You get the idea.

'Why don't you just put in the phones and fill in all those forms afterwards?' Albert asked.

The man, Albert told me, laughed. 'Sure, we couldn't do that!'

'You're doing it from tomorrow morning. And that's the fucking end of it.' And they did.

On the light side was Albert's visit to New York for St Patrick's Day in the early 1990s. We were waiting for him to arrive from the airport into the Fitzpatrick Hotel. And when he did, he greeted the owners and their senior staff before spotting me and a couple of other familiar media faces. He came over to us and leaned close.

'They had fourteen cars and a truck,' he said.

We looked at him.

'They had fourteen cars and a truck in the motorcade from the airport,' he said, clearly impressed by it all.

Finally, here is a story from the peace process.

I always think that the part played by Albert and John Major is overshadowed to a large extent by all the bouquets thrown at Bertie and Blair. But he and Major had a vital role to play in bringing about the Downing Street Declaration of December 1993, precursor to the Good Friday Agreement.

I was told by a former colleague who is 100 per cent reliable that at one tense meeting prior to that agreement being signed, Albert was on one side of the table with his team and John Major on the other with his. Major was nervously fiddling with a pencil when a serious point had been reached in the discussions. Major was thinking.

Albert intervened: 'Don't make a **** of me on this one John.'

The pencil snapped. Major spoke: 'I think we can ask the civil servants to leave and Albert and I will have a chat.'

They did. And peace reigns.

There was also New York in 1994, Ireland versus Italy in Giants Stadium. After the game, Albert Reynolds was there, shaking hands with fans and smiling and...

Well, it was June 18, 1994 and the Loughinisland massacre had just taken place. Six Catholics, watching the game in a local pub, had been murdered by the UVF. Albert clearly hadn't been told. So a few of us journalists pulled him aside and let him know. He nodded gratefully and left.

The Dubliners, The Fureys, Jim McCann and Stockton's Wing

It was the early 1980s, but trying to be precise about dates in that period is difficult. Niall Hanley asked me to go to Holland where Irish acts where heading up a big gig. It was called The Johnny Ross gig. Headlining were: The Dubliners, The Furey Brothers and Davey Arthur, Stockton's Wing, Jim McCann and Drops of Brandy. I remember thinking, 'If this plane goes down, I'll be on page 15.'

Anyway, we made it to Holland. Drink had been consumed in the airport and on the plane. More was consumed on our coach and more that night. It was that kind of trip.

The gig was indoors in front of a massive audience. The morning of it, the Dubliners were on stage – I can't remember where – for a radio interview in front of a live audience. Barney McKenna slept throughout. And because it was live, nobody could wake him up. So the other lads played and sang and talked for the half hour or whatever it was.

As soon as the interview was over, and they were told they were off the air, Ronnie Drew shook Barney and said:

'Barney, Barney. Why were you asleep for the whole interview?'

And he replied, logically: 'Because I was fuckin' tired.' It was that kind of trip.

Later, I was strolling through town, with someone – can't remember who – looking for somewhere to eat. We saw Ronnie alone, sitting at the table in a little restaurant so we went in. We looked at the menu as we chatted with Ronnie.

'The secret to ordering food abroad,' he said, 'is to know what's what and to keep it simple. So I just ordered the steak.'

As he spoke, the waiter arrived with Ronnie's meal and put it down in front of him.

'What the fuck's that?' Ronnie asked him.

'The eels sir. You ordered the eels.'

He threw his eyes to heaven and ordered the steak. It was that kind of trip.

Jim McCann had given it a ferocious lash on the trip over. And he was due on stage after what I would say was more of a coma than a sleep. I was worried for him. No need. He was absolutely magnificent. A superstar. They all were, to be fair.

Late that night, or early the next day, I sat up in the lobby with Steve Cooney and the singer from Drops of Brandy. Steve mesmerized us with his guitar playing, particularly when he played 'Classical Gas' on his own. At three in the morning. In a hotel lobby. In Rotterdam. It was that kind of trip.

Next day, we were heading home and all gathered in Schipol airport. Most were going to Dublin but the Dubliners were heading for Berlin for a big outdoor gig.

I chatted to Luke Kelly for a while. He was, he said, pissed off that doctors had told him to give up drinking for a year because of his ill health. He had collapsed on stage in Cork.

'Turns out it had nothing to do with drink,' he said. 'Waste of a fucking year of my life.'

He was dead within 18 months.

But at the airport, the musicians from all the Irish bands jammed together. What a treat that was for us and anyone passing. Indeed, many didn't pass; they stood and listened.

So enjoyable was it that the Dubliner's missed their flight to Berlin. Desperate attempts were being made to get them there for the gig – 30,000 people were waiting for them.

We just headed home with our memories for a rest and a bit of recovery. It had been that kind of trip.

David Bowie

It was one of those great occasions. It was 1987 and I was on one of what were then regular visits to New York. As ever, I linked up with Muriel Reddy who was living there with her then partner. Muriel and I had become great friends in college – Katherine Donnelly was the third member of our little band. Anyway, on this visit, Muriel did something spectacular. She got me into the press launch of David Bowie's US tour.

It was in the Cat Club in Manhattan and the audience was small and made up, largely, of journalists. After the band had played there was a Q&A. I was at the back and I put my hand in the air and repeatedly asked, 'What about Ireland?'

After about ten minutes, a cameraman from an American TV channel grabbed me by the shoulder. 'Do you mind keeping your fucking hand down? We've been live on the air for ten minutes and all people have seen so far is the back of your fucking hand.'

I put my hand down. As it happens, David answered just then, saying he was very much hoping to make it to Ireland...

Johnny Ronan

I did the odd 'nixer' in my day. Didn't make me rich. One was the opening of Beshoff's chipper on D'Olier Street in Dublin. I had done a little bit of work for Paul McGlade. And he was associated with Paddy McKillen and Johnny Ronan who were behind Beshoff's. Hence my getting the gig.

So. How do you open a fish and chip shop and get publicity? I had a meeting with Johnny and told him my plan. I got the feeling that all would be well. As long as it worked.

Because my plan was to hold the official opening at 7.30 in the morning.

The logic was, simply, that to hold a reception in the evening would pit it against far sexier events. The diary writers would all be out in the evening gathering stuff for their columns. And the chances of a news reporter being sent to cover the opening of a chip shop was zero.

So who in hell would come to the opening of a chip shop at 7.30 in the morning? I had a suspicion that City Manager Frank Feely would come. Frank liked a reception. And one that had nothing to do with wine or sandwiches! Frank liked to get out and meet people. So I asked him. And he accepted the invitation.

And then I promised Johnny I'd get Charlie Haughey to attend. You see, old man Ivan Beshoff was 100 years of age. Charlie used to tell people what a great friend Ivan was. How they got on so well. They may have met on occasion, but 'great friends' was pushing it.

So I called P.J. Mara. 'Would Charlie come to the opening of a fish and chip shop at 7.30 in the morning in a couple of weeks?'

'He will in his arse,' P.J. replied.

'It's Beshoffs. Old man Beshoff will be there.'

'Ya bollocks,' P.J. said. 'Sure how can he not go? Ya bollocks.'

So Charlie was on the team too.

The reception was packed. Novelty as much as anything lured the guests. Fish and chips for breakfast. And the evening newspapers turned up, delighted that they had something fresh, something the dailies didn't have. It got great coverage and I got a little envelope from Johnny containing my, eh, 'professional fee'.

Fr Brian D'Arcy

I hope Fr Brian D'Arcy doesn't mind me telling this story. It was a charity celebrity soccer match between a Dermot Morgan XI and one headed by Dennis Waterman. The game was in UCD. There were many celebs around – I remember big Moss Keane scaring the whatsit out of opposing players. His soccer skills weren't magnificent but God could he roar.

Anyway, I was kind of looking after Dermot's team, he being on the pitch. And at half time I had to take some players off to allow others to get on. One of those I took off was Fr Brian

D'Arcy. A few minutes into the second half, Brian came up beside me and, quietly, asked me why I had taken him off at half time. I knew why. And I told him.

'Because you're a priest, Brian, and I reckoned you were the only one who wasn't going to tell me to fuck off.'

Dennis Waterman and Rula Lenska

It's worth recording that, after the match, we all went to a restaurant in Dun Laoghaire for a meal and a piss-up. Dermot sought me out and asked me to sit at a particular table which I did – on my own for a while.

Then he marched over with Dennis Waterman and his then partner Rula Lenska. There had been something of a tabloid frenzy in England over the couple so I was thinking it was decent of them to come to Dermot's event. And then Dermot pointed at the table I was at.

'Dennis, Rula. You can sit here. This is Paddy. He works for the *Daily Star*.'

They stared at me. They stared at Dermot. They stared at me again.

'Dennis, I'm off duty. I don't give a shite. I don't care what you do, I've no interest. Honestly. You're in Ireland. I'm on the piss.'

He believed me. He actually trusted me I think because I was able to remind him that we'd met before after his *Late Late Show* appearance and that, in my company, he had told a friend who wanted them to go for a meal:

'I told you, in Dublin, no solids.'

I hadn't quoted him! We had a great afternoon.

Ben Bradlee

I had the privilege of meeting legendary *Washington Post* editor Ben Bradlee back in 1980. I was with an NUJ delegation from Independent Newspapers which was looking at what was then 'new technology' in newspapers. The *Post* was one of our destinations.

Ben was brilliant. He showed us around and then, in his office, told his about the new technology. Two of the things he said are memorable. The *Post* had only switched on a couple of days prior to our visit. And so he was able to say this:

'This is the most modern technology currently in use in any newspaper anywhere in the world. And it's completely obsolete.'

He was right on both counts. But more interesting was this:

'The only problem I have is that every five minutes I get a message across the top of my screen saying "Fuck off Bradlee..." and as soon as I find out who's responsible...' He smiled. A bit.

Ben featured large in the brilliant movie *The Post* with Tom Hanks and Meryl Streep. Sadly, no mention in the film of the 'Fuck Off Bradlee' incident.

Phil Orr

I met one of those heroes just after he retired. Phil Orr popped into the Horse and Tram on the night before a game against England. The place was packed. He was, I think, alone. So of course I went over, introduced myself and asked him if he'd like a pint. He said yes. I was thrilled.

So, I wondered, what are you doing now different from what you used to do the night before a big game? Phil said he'd been to a reception in Whiskey Corner. And as he walked up towards the Horse and Tram, he'd popped into a few pubs along the way.

'And in every one, a fuckin' eejit like you bought me a pint.' He was smiling.

A bunch of lads in English jersies were in the corner. 'Do you know them?' he asked me.

I told him I didn't.

'Ah, sure introduce me.'

I did. They couldn't believe their luck, meeting an Irish legend.

'Great to see you Phil,' they said, 'would you like a pint?' He looked over and winked at me.

Mick Jagger

This has nothing to do with newspapers. I was only a child for this particular encounter. I think of the name 'Luggala'. It's a name which brings to mind the beauty of Wicklow, the Guinness dynasty, the Beatles and 'A Day in the Life', their song about Tara Browne, the Rolling Stones and Mick Jagger, Garech Browne and wild parties we never imagined took place on our saintly isle. But they did.

Liam Collins paid a last visit to the estate and wrote a superb piece about it in the *Sunday Indo*. It brought me back 50-something years to the mid-1960s. I was about 12 or 13. I was strolling from Mount Merrion towards Stillorgan, close to Oatlands College, on the old road to Bray. I saw a large car approach. It was a Rolls Royce, moving quite slowly. As it drew close, the back window opened and I saw a man lean across a woman to throw a cigarette butt onto the road. I only saw them for a couple of seconds. The man looked like Mick Jagger and the woman like Marianne Faithful. The window went up slowly. And I looked at the smouldering butt on the ground.

I didn't mention the incident to anyone for years. I mean, Mick Jagger and Marianne Faithful in Stillorgan? I would have been locked up for suggesting such an unlikely occurrence. It was years before I mentioned what I imagined I had seen. To my amazement – and I can't even remember who I was talking to – he said it more than likely was who I thought it was.

'Regular visitors to Luggala,' he said. 'Probably on their way to the airport after a wild weekend.'

After that, I mentioned it to several people I thought might have an informed view. Unanimously, they said it more than likely was Mick Jagger and Marianne Faithful. Two questions remain. Should I have reported him for littering? Or kept the butt as a souvenir?

Laurence Harvey

Laurence Harvey was a brilliant actor. In his short life he managed to marry three times and have numerous affairs, annoy fellow actors and drink and smoke like they were going out of fashion which, in fairness, at least one of them was. In 1972, the year before he died, I had a summer job in a bar in London's Soho. It was called The Crown and Two Chairmen. Good pub. And it's still there. It was, occasionally, packed. And sometimes there would be familiar faces – the film industry had lots of offices in the area at the time.

One of those familiar faces was that of Adam Faith. And another was Laurence Harvey. He'd come in with a few friends and they'd sit in a corner and smoke and drink and laugh for an hour or more before leaving. Nice bunch – they sometimes gave me a tip. One day, after a few weeks of serving them, one of the lads came up to the bar to order a round. And then he asked me a question:

'Paddy,' he said, 'what's your real name.'

I replied, 'It's Paddy.'

He cracked up, turned to Laurence Harvey and the others and said:

'Lads, Paddy's real name is Paddy.'

And they all laughed heartily. And there was me thinking they called me Paddy because we were (kind of) friends. I still like Laurence Harvey even though his friend suggested that calling him 'Larry' just for a laugh might not be a good idea.

Lord Henry Mountcharles

The Stones gig at Slane was memorable. Yes, there had been a gig before with Thin Lizzy, U2 and Hazel O'Connor playing the venue in 1981. But the following year was when it really took off. What was it, 70,000 people? More than twice the number which had been there the previous year. And that previous year's attendance was, I think, a record at the time. Anyway, it was shaping up to be a great day.

James Morrissey and I were lurking around looking for something to do, and probably for something free. We saw people going into the actual castle. Guests of Lord Henry's going in for lunch. Sure, we'll give it a go said James. And in we went. Nobody stopped us.

We followed the crowd into the dining room. Nobody stopped us.

We found a table for two and sat at it. Nobody stopped us.

Great, we thought. Then Henry saw us and marched over.

'Who let these ***** in?' he asked loudly. And then he smiled, said hello to us both and asked if we were having lunch. Amazing reaction.

Even more amazing was that at one point during the Stones' set, I sat with Henry in a living room overlooking the site, and he put on a Pink Floyd album.

'I'd love to have them here sometime,' he said. Sadly, that never happened...

Lemmy

This was a short meeting. It happened on January 9, 1986 in Richmond in Surrey. The occasion was a memorial service for Phil Lynott who had died five days earlier. I was among a crowd outside St Elizabeth's Catholic Church where a service was held for Phil before his body was brought home to Dublin for burial in Sutton cemetery.

There was a strict admission policy in force at the church. And journalists weren't among the invitees. Nor, it seems, was Lemmy from Motorhead. So we ended up chatting, mostly about Phil. Eventually, we shook hands and Lemmy walked away.

Then a journalist, a high profile, highly paid showbiz reporter from a very big English tabloid came up to me, introduced himself and asked: 'Who was that you were talking to? Anyone I should mention?'

God almighty. One of the most recognisable faces in music and this guy hadn't a notion. I told him. I had to spell Lemmy for him. I won't tell you his name. He might still be just as thick and I wouldn't like to embarrass him.

Mick McCarthy

Sardinia 1990. We had just arrived to start coverage of Ireland's adventures in Italia '90. I was working for *The Star*. And just as I arrived at the training ground being used by the Irish squad, I was approached by an agent who was working for the squad.

'Your paper hasn't paid into the players' fund. You can't talk to any of them,' he said.

'But,' I pleaded, 'we've agreed everything. Just a case of the cheque clearing. You know that.'

'You can speak with them when it's cleared. I've told them they are not to talk to anyone from your paper.' He walked away.

I must have looked upset, because next thing Mick McCarthy – who I'd never met before – was standing beside me.

'You okay son? Is there something wrong?'

I explained to him what had happened.

'Are you sure it's all agreed?' he asked me. 'I wouldn't let the other lads down.'

I assured him it was.

'Well, you can talk to me then,' he said.

A gentleman then, and a gentleman always.

Denis Law

It's pushing it to call this a meeting. But I was with Connie in Old Trafford for a United match. We were accompanying two people who had won a competition in *The Star* to go to the match. We were their escorts.

We were eating in one of the restaurants in the ground. Wilf McGuinness came in. Big round of applause. He told a few yarns and went and sat at a table. Paddy Crerand came in. Big round of applause. He waved, signed a few autographs and sat down. One or two other former players arrived. They all got big rounds of applause and sat down.

Then Denis Law came in. Big round of applause? More than that. Once he was spotted everybody stood and cheered and clapped. Still The King. And I got to shake his hand.

Packie Bonner

Not really a meeting either. It was an Irish friendly game at the old Lansdowne Road. And for some reason, a rake of journalists were signed up to take penalties against Packie at half time. I was one of them.

God knows why. Soccer wasn't my game, I'm a rugby man. And I was about three stone overweight! Anyway, my turn came. And believe it or not, I scored. Couldn't believe it.

When it came to my second penalty – we were to take two each – Packie walked up to me.

'I remember what you did the last time,' he said.

And I did too. So I kind of changed my mind on the run up. And kicked it straight at him. He smiled.

Highlight of the day? My colleague Paul Lennon's second penalty. He placed the ball. He walked back. He ran forward. He swung his leg. Packie dived. Packie stood up and looked in the back of the net. The ball wasn't there. He looked left and right. No sign of the ball. He looked in front of him. The ball was still on the spot. Paul had fresh-aired. He'd taken a swipe at the ball and missed. Made my day. And Packie's.

Michael Schumacher

I was in Maranello, the headquarters of Ferrari, as a guest of my friend Eddie Irvine. We got to watch Michael Schumacher practise and chat with the press, a small exclusive bunch of journalists. At the end of the session, a half dozen or so stood on one side of a small barrier and asked Michael questions. Technical questions. Nerdy questions. Show-offy kind of questions. And he turned to go.

'Michael, would you sign an autograph?' I asked. I was thinking of the daughter of a friend.

He kept walking.

'It's for a little girl,' I said, a little louder.

He seemed to hesitate. But kept walking.

'She's very sick,' I said, loudly and untruthfully.

He stopped, turned, came back and signed. Pity I hadn't the correct spelling of the child's name...

Steve Bruce and Eric Cantona

The two United heroes were in Dublin to launch, I think, a testimonial for someone. Anyway, they were in Dobbins and I got chatting to them and they signed autographs for me – once Eric had checked I wasn't going to sell them.

My friend and colleague Brian Farrell – the one who became editor of the *Sunday World*, not the photographer – who actually despises Manchester United then surprised me and said he'd love to have his picture taken with Steve Bruce. So I asked Steve and he said fine. And as Brian stood beside Steve for the picture, I said:

'Steve, Brian is what we call an ABU.'

Steve had clearly never heard of such a thing.

'ABU?' he repeated.

'Yes,' I said. 'Anyone But United.'

Steve and Eric looked at each other, and then they stared at Brian with, I think, a mixture of curiosity and contempt.

So I walked away and left them.

Shane McGowan

Lillies, early 1994. I'm there with a gang from *The Star* and we spot Shane McGowan sitting at a table. So Connie and I, accompanied by Tim Clifford, go over to him for a chat. He was grand. Then I suggested to him that the ideal anthem for that summer's World Cup in the US would be 'Thousands are Sailing'. Tim suggested that Shane could write the music and

I'd do the words. Neither of us realised it was a Phil Chevron song. Maybe Shane did though as he told us to fuck off...

Eddie Irvine

Eddie invited me to go to Italy, to a ski resort where the entire Ferrari outfit was spending a week. Great opportunity.

I don't ski but I fancied myself at apres ski and reckoned the whole thing would be fun. In fact, I nearly took skiing lessons. I was told where they'd be and at what time. So I just looked out of the window of my room to check that teacher and students were all there. They were. And the oldest 'student' I could see was about six so I decided to skip it.

I was delighted Eddie asked me. I wouldn't call us friends. But still, it was a nice thing to do, one Irish journalist and it was me. On the first evening we were sitting together in the hotel bar when an English journalist approached and asked Eddie if he could have a few words.

'I'm doing a thing with Paddy at the moment,' he said.

The same thing happened the following morning with another journalist. And again that evening. So I decided to say something.

'Eddie, you can talk to those other lads if you want. I mean, I'm not actually interviewing you. You're not just using me to get rid of them are you?'

'Why the fuck do you think I asked you?' he said smiling.

And I still had to buy the next round. But he's a good mate.

The proof of that came when Connie had her first brain haemorrhage. She was in Beaumont Hospital for weeks on end. And there were cards coming in from all and sundry in the sports world. Flowers too in some cases. All really thoughtful. Connie knew all these people from her job – Sports Editor of *The Star*, the first female sports editor in Ireland and, indeed,

131

voted by her peers as Sports Editors' Sports Editor in the In Dublin Awards.

Anyway, there she was in Beaumont when who arrives at her bedside but Eddie Irvine. He had bothered to drive to the hospital, get parking and find where she was to sit by her bed for half an hour. It was a really decent thing to do and a measure of the man.

How famous was he back then? For the next week, almost everyone who walked past Connie's room pointed at it and you could actually hear some of them say, 'That's where he was...'

Harry Crosbie

Harry Crosbie is known to most Dubliners as the man who gave us Vicar Street, the Point as it was and the whole Bord Gais Energy Theatre Grand Canal Dock thing. It started with The Point.

A friend suggested an interview with Harry as he began the work of converting what had been an old railway station into a concert venue. In the docks. In a part of Dublin hardly any one, other than dockers, ever visited. I stood with him in the vast expanse of the empty station as he described what he planned to do and how he was going to fill the place with concert goers. I looked at him.

'You think I'm a fuckin' eejit, don't you?'

I said nothing.

'Watch. The city will come down here to meet me,' he said.

I didn't believe a word of it. But he was right!

Rosemary Smith

I was assigned to the *Sunday Independent* for a few years in the seventies. They carried a kind of gossip column called 'Backchat'. So when I saw the rally driver Rosemary Smith advertising her house for sale just over the border in County Meath, saying it was '15 minutes from O'Connell Street'. I wrote a smartarse piece for Backchat suggesting it might be 15 minutes for Rosemary Smith but...

She called on the Tuesday when we were back in the office. She invited me down to her house. She was charming. We had a cup of coffee and then she said we were going for a drive.

'Note the time,' she said.

And off we went. We pulled up a while later at O'Connell Bridge. It was just under 15 minutes since we'd left her house in County Meath and she never broke the speed limit! Of course I wrote a piece putting it right. But I couldn't get over how good-humoured she was about it. Most people would have been furious.

A wonderful lady. And a brilliant driver!

Dominic Behan

Dominic Behan, Brendan's equally talented brother, wrote a column in the *Evening Herald* for a few years. It generally came through me, though rarely did a word of it have to be changed. He could write just as well as he could compose songs!

Anyway, one Christmas those of us who worked in the features department in the *Herald* decided we'd have our Christmas lunch in the Indo canteen. So about ten or twelve of us gathered, lashed into the wine and ate the grub. We were, I think you could say, 'nicely' by mid-afternoon.

Then who should drop in but Dominic Behan. So I chatted with him, my boss, Features Editor Colm McGinty chatted with him, and then someone asked him if he'd sing for us what is probably his best known song, 'Liverpool Lou'.

He said he would. And then he began to explain to us how he came to write the song. I was thinking what a privilege this is, Dominic Behan is not only going to sing 'Liverpool Lou' for us, he's going to tell us how and why he wrote it. And then someone spoke. (I won't name the speaker because he is still a friend and I wouldn't like to embarrass him. So Colm McGinty needn't worry!)

'Ah Dominic, would you just sing the fuckin' song,' he said. Dominic stopped talking. And he did sing the 'fuckin' song. And it was a rare privilege.

Sir John Leslie

We visited Castle Leslie quite often. On one particular visit, we noticed Sir John Leslie leading a couple of people up the stairs and figured it was one of his impromptu tours of the Castle for which he was known. So we joined in.

It was fine and interesting – except for the ignorant American who was carrying a glass of something or other and had clearly consumed a load before going on the tour. He kept making stupid comments and asking stupid questions. Sir John had just pointed out to us Winston Churchill's Christening robe when the Yank interjected with a disparaging question.

'Did you know Winston Churchill?' he slurred.

Sir John looked at him and said: 'His mother and my grandmother were sisters,' and went back to the tour. It was the most polite fuck off I had ever heard.

Mind you, I wasn't so pleased with Sir John the next morning. I was sitting drinking coffee and reading newspapers while the ladies had some kind of treatment in the spa. I had the *Irish Independent* in my hands and my copy of *The Irish Times* was on the table in front of me. Sir John happened along.

'May I have a look at your newspaper?' he asked.

'Certainly,' I said.

He picked it up, folded it under his arm and walked away. I stared after him and then noticed the other men sniggering. It seemed, it was a trick he often pulled on unsuspecting guests!

PART 2 – BACK TO THE BEGINNING ...

I was born on August 5, 1953 in the Cascia Nursing home on Pembroke Street. My mother had a mastectomy a year or so prior to my birth – and she survived another 50 years.

Spinning Coins

My first memory is of sitting in a high chair in the house on Sycamore Road in Mount Merrion watching in awe as my sister Aileen was spinning coins on the tray in front of me. Why I should remember that and not other things that happened while I was a baby and a toddler I don't know.

A Big Job

It was many years before I could hear people talking about a Big Job and not snigger. In our house nobody did a Number Two. Nobody did a Poo. They did Big Jobs.

As a toddler, if I emerged from the toilet – it was long before they became loos – my mother would ask if I had done a Big Job or a Wee Wee. Indeed, there were many occasions when I had to inform her that I needed to do a Big Job in a hurry.

In later years, my older brothers and sisters confirmed that they too had been through years of Big Jobs and Wee Wees. The result was that when, slightly older, I heard someone had been given a Big Job in London, or if I was informed that they were going to do a Big Job on the parish hall, or that there was a Big Job available in New York, I smiled to myself.

My Pals

I had a number of little friends when I was a very young child. They were my best friends. We never fought. We never fell out. And, boy, did we have adventures. The three friends were: Andy Kandoodenhop, Jimmy Cazawalla and Terry Flower who was, as it happens, a tortoise. You have probably figured out already that they lived, largely, in my head.

The names? Well, I haven't a clue. It has been suggested that Andy and Jimmy's surnames at least, came from orders I had heard barked out, in Irish, at the barracks in which my Uncle Gerard was stationed. I don't know. But I am pretty sure my Uncle's influence is why Terry the tortoise served in the Congo with the Irish Army. Really.

Mount Merrion

I cannot imagine a better place to grow up than in Mount Merrion, that middle class south Dublin suburb often described as 'leafy' because it was. And Sycamore Road was a magical place. And our house was the best in Mount Merrion because that's where we lived!

My father had paid £525 for it in 1939. He would have bought a detached house nearby but he couldn't raise the extra £50. For a while, it was Mammy and Daddy in one room, Donal in the small room, Aileen and Una in one of the big bedrooms and Dee, John and I in the other.

I was four years younger than the next youngest, John. And that means I had more time on my own with my mammy than the others did. A request to 'take Patrick out with you' would result in my brothers dashing out the door at record speed. Teenagers bringing little brothers out with them wasn't, and still isn't, the done thing.

My mother collected me from school in my first few years, then called Low Babies and High Babies. Then, when I reached First Class I'd walk home on my own and we'd play hot and cold, which meant me looking for my treat which she had always hidden somewhere in the kitchen, telling me I was 'getting warmer' if I got close and 'getting colder' if I was going in the wrong direction.

I remember sometimes sitting on her knee in the living room, listening to BBC Radio (Radio Éireann shut down at 2.00 or 2.30 every day), and looking out into the garden. I still remember that time very well.

When I was very young, I gave my first hint of what was to be a lifelong career in newspapers. I produced the *Daily Midget*, a hand drawn newspaper which I sold to my father. He was chairman and CEO of the ESB and had to deal, constantly, with strikes. And even as a toddler I couldn't help but be aware that his was a tough job. But that didn't stop the *Daily Midget* going on strike one day. In this instance, but not in the ESB, Daddy capitulated and gave in to my demands. As far as I recall, he had to cough up six pence.

Later in Willow Park I worked on one of the school newspapers (there were rival publications even in primary school), the *Willow Bugle*, but I had to leave over editorial differences. I wanted humour in it. The editor didn't.

Mount Merrion was wonderful. And we had wonderful neighbours. As children, we thought our neighbours were fine. Quiet, some of them. Other more outgoing. But fine. But we discovered later in life that two close neighbours had committed suicide, of which, at the time, we were utterly unaware, protected by parents who were, well, very protective.

But for us, it was a happy place. We played on the road and in the woods near the church. Now, those woods are manicured to an extent but then they were a place which was untamed. We spent many Saturday afternoons in the Stella cinema. We got our bikes fixed by Mr Rothery who should have been a millionaire – he had the first petrol pump on the Dublin to Bray/Rosslare road!

Haircuts were in Bauman's and you'd see Mr Bauman strutting around in his jodhpurs, nick nacks came from Lloyds, newspapers from McCarry's, meat from McDonaghs, groceries from Findlaters, delivered of course, clothes cleaned by IMCO or Prescott's, O'Shea's was our chemist, Mr Lennon fixed our shoes.

Dr Reggie Spellman was our doctor until we changed to Dr Margaret Daly. Reggie liked a drink. And sometimes he might have one or two before seeing patients. An excellent doctor, but I think my Pioneer parents decided we should change. And so it was off to Dr Daly. She looked after our medical needs, day and night. Mr Cribben was our dentist but best not go there. Popular he wasn't.

And even from seven or eight, I could walk to them all, across that main road. I even saw a car on it now and then!

The Church Collection

Sometimes I was asked to stand at the door of the Church of St Therése in Mount Merrion to help with the collection. In those days, a wooden dish sat on a table and, as people came in the door, they put money into the dish. Generally, it was a few pennies or sixpences. The odd donor put in a half crown. And every now and then, you'd see a ten shilling note. Sometimes, the people putting in the ten shilling notes made a bit of a thing of it. Some, though, would show me the ten shilling note, or even a pound note, put it in and take a bit of change.

One man, in particular, certainly did. I have no idea who he was. But on almost every single occasion that I was on duty he put a ten shilling note into the dish and took out five half crowns – which was 12/6. I was a kid. He was an adult. I could not say or do anything. Occasionally, he made a big show of not taking any change, but he was a thief. And I couldn't stop him.

The Accident

I was about seven or eight, sitting on a bench near the bus stop opposite Willow Park School in Booterstown, waiting for the Number 5 bus to take me home. It was, I think, autumn or winter. It was dusk. Suddenly a quite noisy, old fashioned motorbike was heading away from the junction and towards me. Neither he, nor I, saw the old man crossing the road. I didn't even hear the bike hit him. I just heard the silence after he did. The old man lay on his back. There was blood around his head. He was dead. I had never seen anyone dead. But I knew he was. The motorcyclist was sitting on the bench a little away from me, helmet beside him, head in his hands. I hadn't even seen him walk from his bike to the bench. It was as if time had stood still. Some cars moved slowly towards the scene. Some people walked towards the dead old man.

But I just got up and ran. I ran like I had never run before. I ran the whole way home, a mile, maybe a little more. And I didn't stop running until I was being held by my mother and I blurted out what I had seen. I know she gave me sweet tea to calm me, but really I remember little else. It was never mentioned again, at home or at school. But it burned deep, very deep. It was my first encounter with death.

Extraordinarily, twice more I saw people knocked down and killed. In Bray, I saw a girl run diagonally across the road.

By the time she was half way across, she had her back to the traffic. So she didn't see the car heading down the hill. It struck her and she fell to the ground. Later, I heard she had died.

Some years later, I was in town, on Westmoreland Street, when I heard the screech of brakes. A large, articulated truck had come to a halt outside what is now Starbucks. I looked back and 100 metres behind the truck lay the body of an elderly man who had been struck. Three people knocked down and killed, and I saw them all die.

My Rugby Career

I played rugby from the age of seven until I was fourteen. Then I left it behind for a decade. Why? Laziness, bad attitude and probably just not being good enough. But I remember my first try very, very well.

We were playing St Mary's on the front pitch in Rathmines. It was the Under 8s. It was snowing but the game went on. And, eventually, I got over their line right in the right hand corner as you look at the school buildings. The referee – a priest from St Mary's – awarded the try. Then he hesitated and wondered whether or not I hadn't gone over the dead ball line which was covered in snow. But he eventually left it go and gave the try.

I point it out every time I pass the ground even if I'm with Connie and she's heard me say the same thing over and over a thousand times. Yes, I know great players like Johnny Sexton have graced that pitch. But I really feel sad that there's no plaque marking my first ever try.

'On this spot, Paddy Murray, playing for Willow Park Under 8s, may or may not have scored his first ever try.'

I was pretty good at it in Willow Park. I played on all the teams from the Under 8s up to the Under 12s, with the exception of the Under 11s when I was in Ring. Embarrassingly, there was one terrible moment on the Under 8s when I was sent off. Yes, sent off in an Under 8s game. Why? The other team scored and we stood under the posts for the conversion. As we stood there, I noticed all the chestnuts – conkers to us – on the ground and began to pick a few up. I didn't notice the rest of the team running to the half way line for the kick off. Brother Luke, our trainer, summoned me.

'If you're more interested in collecting chestnuts than playing the game, you may as well go and get changed.'

Sent off. And it's not even an offence in the laws of rugby to collect chestnuts during a game. I checked.

I didn't get my place on the Under 13s which was disappointing. But the following year, up in the College, I played almost every game for the Under 14s bar a few I missed when I hurt my back falling from a tree on a scout trip to Powerscourt. I had hoped to make the Junior Cup Team the following year, but from very early on Fr 'Nudie' Boyle made it clear I wasn't going to make it. He dropped me, hinting that there was nothing I could do to get back in the team. I was dropped. Permanently.

So there ended my rugby career, almost. Fast forward to 1973. The week before I started in the *Indo* I went to London to visit my brother John. I had a few things to do and people to meet in London. I got to Bowie's concert in the Hammersmith Odeon. I had a few drinks some of the nights. And more than a few on others, including the night before I was to take part in a Sevens event at London Irish.

I togged out. Me in a London Irish rugby jersey. Proud as punch. And hungover. I tried. I really did. But it didn't take long for them to figure out that I was suffering. So after one game, I gave up.

An ignominious end to a career? Eh, no. That was yet to come twenty years later, playing for the Golden Oldies from CYM in Terenure. That happened because my editor at *The Star*, Michael Brophy, asked me to meet a guy from CYM, the sports club next door to our offices.

'It's a guy called Michael Croke. He wants us to do something with his golden oldies rugby team. Do what you have to do. But no money.'

Several thousand euro later the tournament took place. Yes indeed, I promised money for this that and the other and we even produced a souvenir programme from *The Star* offices.

The tournament was brilliant. It was a joy to play rugby again. We won our first two games and I was given the honour of captaining the team in the final game. But I was sent off again!

This time, it was for suggesting to the Australian referee who was officiating in our game against Australian opposition that he was a tad biased, though I may not have been quite that polite. My last action on a rugby field was walking off with my head hung low. I wasn't ashamed. I was looking for chestnuts. And, by the way, I was right. He was biased.

'Oh Perish Those Who Would So Serious Be'

We had decided that our logo for the tournament would be a chicken waving a white flag and our motto would be, 'Fuck 'em if they can't take a joke'.

Only we all agreed that proper mottos should be in Latin. So I asked my colleague Senan Molony if he could somehow get those words translated into Latin. Senan got on to the classics department in Oxford University and asked them if it could be done.

Much to my surprise, a few days later Senan came to me and said he had the Latin motto for me.

'I got on to Oxford,' he said, 'and they told me the closest they could find was a quote from the playwright Plautus who, in the second century BC wrote: *'Pereant quem severi'*, which means, 'Oh perish those who would so serious be'.

So that's what we had stitched onto our jackets!

Mr President

Odd how things turn out. Just over 20 years after Michael Croke managed to get me to stump up several thousand euro of *The Star's* money, he asked me if I would be willing to serve as Vice President of CYM – by this stage renamed Terenure Sports Club. Vice President. It sounded okay. Didn't seem that onerous. Only as soon as I said yes and was in situ, he revealed that there wasn't actually a candidate for president, so…

Two year I spent as President of that club. No big deal? Multi sports club in South Dublin? What was the problem?

Well, an example was one day when I was having a treatment in St James' Hospital. It was nothing too invasive so I planned to read a book. Only during the two hours I was on that chair, I sent or received 32 emails about club business. Who could have imagined it involved negotiating with the Irish Music Rights Organisation among other things?

Thing is, I enjoyed it. I enjoyed the two years. And I don't think I left any permanent damage behind.

Frank Left Comedy Behind

You may be familiar with the name Frank Connolly who has been associated with trade unions, republican and socialist causes certainly since he left school, probably before that. A handy rugby player. But also a comedian.

Yes. Three words you don't see in the same sentence often. Frank Connolly comedian.

Frank and I were a double act. In Willow Park we would perform for the other students. Our act was comedic – and rhyming. And probably bloody awful. I think Frank made the right choice and gave it up. I should have done the same thing.

The 'Millionaires'

You would think we were millionaires. There we were, in our semi-D in Mount Merrion, and for a period of time we had a live-in maid, a gardener and a cleaning lady. But it was the same for everyone else on the road, everyone in the area.

I have no recollection of the live-in maid who left when I was very young. Clever girl, she got out before I made her life hell! Mr Kirwan was the gardener and Mrs Whelan was the cleaning lady. Before she arrived, every week, my mother cleaned the house thoroughly. That was the way of it.

The Stammer

Air travel back in the 1950s wasn't like it is now. Dublin airport was small. Flights were infrequent and visits to the airport were equally so.

My mother had relatives in Manchester, her sister may have been there in the 1950s, her cousin certainly was. And so she was going for a visit. My father brought her to the airport and I was brought to say goodbye. Back then, you could almost park outside the door!

Mammy kissed me and off she went through departures to get on her plane, probably a Viscount! Some time later, I can't remember if we were home or on the way, daddy pointed to a plane overhead.

In Dobbins covering the visit of Steve Bruce and Eric Cantona

With Albert Reynolds in the newsroom

Being presented with a bike for raising most money on a charity cycle
with, on the left, future Indo Managing Editor Michael Denieffe

In Dublin feature with people who would present programmes on
Radio Ireland. I'm on the extreme right and my co-presenter,
Liam Mackey, is third from left

Me with the clear redness of cutaneous lymphoma

A red-faced me with Jeremy Guscott (left) and Joe Dolan (right)

The Editors: Me, Sunday Tribune; Colm McGinty, Sunday World;
Ger Colleran, The Star; and Vinnie Doyle, the Independent

This was the last occasion all six of us were photographed
together. We just happened to be in my sister Úna's house.
(L to R) Aileen, Dee, Donal, Úna, John and me.

The committee to raise funds for paralysed Ciaran McCarthy – the author is far left, top row, Irish rugby international Keith Wood is bottom right and England's Jeremy Guscott is bottom row, second from left.

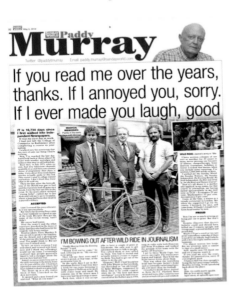

The last column in the Sunday World

The plaque commemorating the Beatles' performance at the Adelphi Cinema

*Lord Mayor Nial Ring, Gay Byrne and me at the
unveiling of the Beatles' plaque in 2018*

A note from Yoko Ono

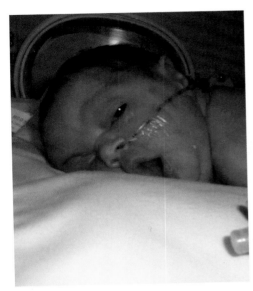

Charlotte at one week old (left) and at our wedding in 2008 (right)

With Connie at last gig – Paul Weller – before Covid

The women I love: On holiday with Charlotte and Connie (above left);
Charlotte the Teen (above right), and Connie and Charlotte (below)

'There's mammy's plane,' he said. 'Mammy's up there on her way.' Or words to that effect.

Now, it's likely that five-year-olds don't have much notion about perspective or scale. Because when daddy told me that my mammy was inside that tiny little dot, I got the fright of my life ... and a hesitation in my speech. It wasn't quite a stammer, but for a while, a few years I'm told, when I spoke my mouth would open, I would try to say the word, and for a few seconds, nothing would come out. It disappeared in the end, probably due to elocution in school or some such thing.

Just shows you though. It's easy to scare the living daylights out of a toddler.

The Brat

I wasn't what you might call a good student. Brat may be the word which comes to mind. I suppose I first demonstrated that (though nobody was to know for a generation) in fourth class in Willow Park. Miss Woods was one of our teachers. She put a chart on the wall on which were listed all of her students' names. When it was merited, she would reach into her bag and take one star from her little box of multi-coloured sticky back stars and put it on the chart beside the recipient's name. Whoever had the most stars by the end of the second term was to be awarded an Easter egg. I was doing okay. Second to the class genius. But second.

Did you know, that in 1963, the Nimble Fingers hobby shop in Stillorgan sold little boxes of sticky back multi coloured stars? I did. I wasn't bad enough to win it outright with my little box of stars. Instead, we were joint winners, the genius and I. And we both got Easter eggs.

A Year in Ring

That less than ideal student had actually started out on the right course. I went into second class in Willow Park at just six years of age and I did okay. Better than okay. I topped the class in a few subjects. I liked learning. And I wasn't bad in third and fourth classes either. But...

My mother and father were told that if I kept going the way I was, I would be just 16 when doing the Leaving Cert in 1970. It had been heard of for girls, very occasionally, to do the Leaving at 16. But never a boy.

It was recommended that, for my own good, I be held back a year. And so I was to do fourth class again. I was told but it didn't really register. Not, at least, until I went to the window of the book shop in the school to get my books.

'Patrick Murray. You're in Fourth Class again,' the Brother said handing me my books.

I took them and went straight to the toilets and locked myself in a cubicle and cried until I could cry no more. Fourth class again. With little kids. And all my friends a year ahead of me now. They wouldn't talk to me. They wouldn't be my friends anymore. It was, up to then, the worst thing that ever happened to me.

Oh yes, done with the best of intentions. Done for the right reasons. But God, it hurt, it really did. I got over it. I got on with it. But I became a different child. That short attention span of mine kicked in and I became the class messer. That's probably why I ended up in the Irish College in Ring, County Waterford, for a year.

It was a horrible year. Long walks every day. Letters home read and checked to make sure they contained no criticism. And the Friday soup! We called it Cheffie's Vomit. It was made by taking all the left over vegetables from the week and boiling them in milk. Uggh! And the beatings. I never suffered them, but I saw them. They were worst in the evenings when some of the teachers returned from an afternoon's boozing.

I have no idea what motivated my parents to send me there. They obviously had no ideas of the horrors it held. I think it was probably their love of the Irish language. And love of me too, I suppose. But for me, my love of them made it all the worse. I missed them, and my brothers and sisters and friends, terribly. I was desperately homesick for the entire year. I probably cried every night.

My mother used to tell people that 'Patrick spent a year in Ring and he loved it'.

I didn't, I hated it. I have no idea why she thought otherwise, God bless her. We dropped in for a visit in about 2016 and it felt a lot different. I surprised myself by conversing with one of the staff entirely in Irish. Funny how my dislike for Ring didn't dent my love for the Irish language. I'd say now though it's the modern, happy school I wish it had been in 1964.

And when the year was over and I went back to Willow Park it was worse again. My friends hadn't spent the year missing me as I had them. They had gotten on with it, made new friends, welcomed new boys to the school. And my place on the rugby team was gone and I never really got it back. Rugby, the other love of my life.

Ring was, effectively, the other woman. It broke us up. Two things done out of love which hurt and hurt. And if I had been bold enough to say how much staying back the year and going to Ring actually hurt, my wonderful mammy and daddy would have undone the damage in an instant. But I wasn't.

JFK in Dublin

It was June 1963, I was nine. We knew, of course, all about JFK. He was the first Irish President of the United States, we were told (of course he wasn't), and the first Catholic (he was!). So the idea of him coming to Ireland was exciting to say the least. I went to see him and I believe it was three times in total.

The first, I think, was as he entered the Dáil. I had cycled in – without permission of course – with a schoolfriend. I saw JFK leaving Dublin Castle too. Then there was the garden part for him at Áras an Úachtaráin. We listened to that on the radio and heard them describing the clothes the women were wearing.

They mentioned my mammy, 'Mrs Maureen Murray, wife of the chairman of the ESB, Tom Murray, wearing a lovely blue summer dress...' and so on. We told her when she got home. She was mortified.

Dev's Dead

It was November 22, 1963. Some of the family were gathered in front of our (fairly new) television (my parents didn't like the word 'telly') watching *The Thin Man*, starring Peter Lawford. The sound went. And then screen went blank.

For some reason, I said: 'De Valera's dead.'

A minute or two later newsreader Charles Mitchell appeared to tell us, tearfully, that President John F Kennedy had been shot dead in Dallas. I was told to tell my brothers who were 'studying' in the kitchen. They believed me only because I used the word 'assassination' , a big one for a ten year old.

I then had to run to the church where I told Father Devine the news and he interrupted Benediction to tell his congregation. I mentioned what was on television, by the way, because the programme starred Peter Lawford, who was JFK's brother-in-law.

No Smoke Without the Nook

He'd end up in jail now, but Mr Lysaght ran the little sweet shop opposite the Booterstown Avenue entrance to Willow Park. We'd head there after school every day. For sweets? Not at all. He sold cigarettes individually. I think it was one penny and a half per cigarette. Churchman's, I think. We could have been no more than 12. But that was the way of things.

The Leaving Cert

My misbehaviour in school continued unabated through secondary, resulting in being suspended three times in fifth year. Even in her last years my mother occasionally reminded me that 'you were the only one we had to go down to the school about'.

Anyway, I did nothing to prepare for the Leaving other than cram in the last few days. So when it came to get the results, I was a little fearful. My father came with me. And when I opened the envelope, we saw that I had gained two honours. My face lit up. His dropped. Different expectations.

Academics

I never really studied hard. Academics wasn't my thing, though I managed to get through exams (until it came to Commerce in UCD). I thought the Inter Cert a doddle at the time. And it probably was back then. Indeed, I finished the honours history paper in an hour and sat back. Then I heard: 'Pssst. Pssst,' coming from behind. It was my classmate Nip.

Nip would not have been a history scholar or a scholar of much of anything. He suggested, by gesture, that I do his paper too. So I took it and I did his exam for him, making sure the answers were sufficiently different from my own.

That Autumn the results came out. I had done pretty well in almost everything, including a B on the honours history paper.

'What did you get in the history?' Nip asked me holding his own results.

'B,' I said.

'You bastard,' he said.

'Why?' I asked. 'Don't tell me I failed it for you.'

'No,' he said angrily. 'You only got me a C.'

There's gratitude for you.

Nicknames

I have been through quite a few nicknames in my life. I can tell you only about the ones I am familiar with, not the ones muttered behind my back or out of earshot!

When I first went to Willow Park, Fr Stanley, 'Stanno', asked me what I wanted to be.

'I want to be the Pope,' I apparently told him. 'But I think I'll be a bishop first.' And so I was called The Bishop.

In Ring, at the Irish College, I was, for reasons which have been lost in the mists of time, known as Murky Cow.

Fr O'Rourke used to call me Murrier the Gurrier during rugby training. I trust this was because I demonstrated toughness and for no other reason.

In the scouts, my nickname was Scrufín. I did not earn this nickname. It was given to me because my brother John, who was also a scout, rarely arrived with an ironed neckerchief and earned the name Scruff. As his younger brother, I became Scrufín.

Later in life, in my last year in 'Rock and for a little while afterwards, I was known as Binge. I would rather not go into why.

My colleague Charlie Mallon in the *Indo* believed, for some reason, that I couldn't keep a secret. 'Telephone, telegram, tell Murray,' he used to say. And he christened me 'Cavemouth'. We remain friends!

We had all heard of Stanno before we entered the doors of Willow Park back in 1960. It wasn't the most imaginative of nicknames for Fr Stanley, the dean. Cockeye, Fr Coughlan, wasn't any more imaginative but there was some thought given to Miss Donagh's name. She was universally known as Ma Donagh because of the way she went on and Fr O'Connor was Paddy Fart because, well, because he was notorious for lifting one cheek of his bum off his chair during class and farting. Mr O'Byrne was Billio – I presume his name was William or Bill. Mr Curtain, the Holy Ghost prefect was JC.

The names in 'Rock itself, a big secondary school, were a bit more grown up. Well, a tiny bit.

Echo, Mr Irwin, was so called because he was quite short, the echo of the other teachers. The Major earned his name because he walked around like an army officer, papers under his arm like a swagger stick. Another military name was Little Hitler, Fr Lodge, but that was more to do with his authoritarian attitude. His alternative nickname was Piss Lodge. Sneaky Jones was actually Fr Ryan who earned his moniker by falling from a small height and damaging a leg whilst spying on the boys in the Jubilee Hall, scene of the college musicals. Speaking of which, the dean, Fr Corless, was known as Bing, after Mr Crosby, because of his love of singing.

John Waldron drove an MGBGT and so was called Flash. Buddy did nothing to earn his name, other than to be Fr Holly, and Dickie Powell was simply called Dickie after an American actor who had passed on long before our group hit his classroom. Brother Bones was thin. Samson was a big man.

Birdie O'Hanlon was called after the character in the *Kennedys of Castleross*, RTÉ's daytime radio soap. And Sandy was strawberry blond. Structure used that word quite a lot in biology class and Glen Ford was, for reasons none of us thought obvious, named after the movie star. Mr McDonald was, of course, Farmer; Rinse had a grey streak in his otherwise black hair; Pop was a father figure in our final year and Buts seemed to begin every sentence with the word but, much as people use 'so' these days.

Grown up nicknames. Other than that given to a young female teacher in our final year. She was the only female teacher of Sixth year students. She was young, pretty, brilliant at her job and very brave. So we gave her a nickname which clearly distinguished her from her male colleagues. Tits, we called her. She took over from Benji who was from the country. His name came from the character in *The Riordans* on RTÉ. Tits was a brilliant teacher and saved a lot of us from a bad result in the Leaving Cert, ensuring, in fact, that many of us got the Honours we wanted and in some cases needed.

And when we walked out the gates of 'Rock for the last time, we finally began to grow up!

Daddy

If I had been let choose my parents, I would have chosen the ones I had. My daddy was wise and loving and funny and fair and principled and strict and soft. If I had only listened to his advice more, I would have been better off. The little bits of advice I *did* take stood to me.

He was a great singer and introduced us to classical music, as well as the songs of Percy French.

Daddy had the maddest sense of humour. Two of his 'riddles': 'Why is a mouse when it spins? Because the higher the fewer.' And: 'What's the difference between a duck? There's no difference. Because each of its legs is both the same.'

He often came home from work with intricate designs, doodles, on his notepad.

Daddy went to 8.00 am Mass every morning without fail. He came home from Mass and brought mammy up a cup of tea in bed before she'd get up and go to 10.00 Mass.

He was a modest man. Chairman and CEO of the ESB. Chairman of the Blood Transfusion Board. Chairman of the Nuclear Energy Board. He believed in public service.

Daddy often brought us to his birthplace of Templederry in Tipperary. When he was a child, the family had run a shop, but now his brother John ran a farm where we often stayed. And we'd visit his sister Nellie (Eileen) who, with her husband Tony, ran a shop in Nenagh. Or his brother Dan who had a farm in Croom in Limerick where we also stayed.

His brother Jim was headmaster in Newbridge College, Paddy a priest in Dublin's Inner City and then Blackrock and his sister Sara a nun in Kells, County Meath.

I remember so well our family holidays in places like Skerries, Rush, Loughshinny, Ardamine and Rosslare. Being the youngest, I holidayed with just mammy and daddy as the others got older. The last holiday I had with them was in the North! Why we went north around the time of the Twelfth – we watched the parade in Portrush – I don't know. But I remember walking across the Carrick-a-Rede Rope Bridge.

I remember meeting a sister of my grand uncle Alec. He had been cut off by his family when he converted to Catholicism to marry my Auntie Aggie. He was tactile. When we were young, we used to hug him every evening when he came home from work. And I loved to rub my soft little cheek against his five o'clock shadow when he came in from work. We were a 'kissy' family. Male or female, we kissed our mammy and daddy when we met them.

Daddy and I often swam together on our holidays. Lord, weren't they the great days? He brought me to the All Ireland Hurling Final of 1964 which, of course, Tipperary won. It was a present before being dispatched to Ring for a year.

Daddy was generous to a fault. He was well paid, but rarely did he and mammy have a decent holiday. Nothing, really, bar the odd trip to the States to see mammy's sister Una. Everything was for us.

I didn't go and see daddy in St Vincent's Hospital the day he died. I probably could have. But I was too frightened. We had seen him deteriorate. He became thinner and thinner and used to sit in a hardback chair sipping Woodward's Gripe Water from the lid of the bottle. It was all he could digest.

Now? Now I see him, sitting in his armchair in the evening, or having a ten minute snooze after lunch. I see him with a Christmas hat on, dishing out the presents from under the tree. I see him at the wheel of his car. I see him at the dinner table. I see him at Mass. I hear him coming in to wake me in the morning after bringing a cup of tea up to my mammy.

Would I go and visit him on that last day if I could turn back time? Would I do it instead of winning the lottery? In a flash.

He retired from the ESB in 1974 but kept on the other two, largely voluntary, jobs at the Nuclear Energy Board and the Blood Transfusion Board, until he died in November 1978.

In February the following year, there was a discussion in the Senate about the ESB. And Senator Gordon Lambert paid a very pointed compliment to my late father, for the enormous work he had done. This is from the report of that discussion:

Senator Lambert: As far as top management are concerned,
I should like to take the opportunity to pay a short tribute
to the late Dr. Tom Murray who headed the organisation
during their time of greatest expansion and unprecedented
social change. He was a man totally concerned with the wel-
fare of our largest organisation. He was a most conscientious
man and a man of great integrity. Indeed, I am proud to be
able to recall his commitment to his great responsibilities and
his dedicated service to the ESB and his fellow men.

We are fortunate that he has been succeeded in recent years
by such a triumvirate of business and technical expertise em-
braced by the Chairman, Professor Charles Dillon, the Chief
Executive, Jimmy Kelly, and Assistant-Chief Executive Paddy Moriarty.

Three people. It took three highly qualified people to replace my father in the ESB. And it took two more to replace
him at the Nuclear Energy Board and the Blood Transfusion
Service. He was, as they say these days, some man for one man!

My sister Una came across an edition of *The Pioneer* magazine which carried an interview with Daddy, a lifelong Pioneer, or teetotaller, just a month before he died. Among other
things, he said this:

In 1960, the ESB seemed to be a stable, placid organization.
In 1961, the first strike took place. Looking back we know
that what happened in the sixties was a social revolution.
The trade union classes, for want of a better word, formed a
different view of their role and they staked their claim. Their
cause was proper. There was an unjust division between blue
collar and white collar workers, and it had to go. You can't
make an omelette without breaking eggs, but I'm speaking
with hindsight now, at the beginning we didn't really know
what was going on.

He was way ahead of his time, a man of vision, as you would expect from someone appointed by Sean Lemass and working in tandem with T.K. Whitaker.

And it was he who signed the documents to build the Poolbeg Chimneys and the innovative Turlough Hill power station – the biggest battery in the world. He brought me there while it was being constructed and we visited again a few years ago. It would not be built now. But it *is* as useful now as it ever was.

Mammy

I used to go into my mammy's bedroom in the morning and give her a kiss before heading off to school. She would be drinking the cup of tea daddy brought up to her before getting up and going to Mass. I remember sitting on her knee listening to the radio – must have been BBC's *Listen with Mother* – with the French doors open and it was just heaven.

Mammy was very clever. She came first in Maths in Ireland at University but never worked. She married in 1939 and in those days married women couldn't work in the civil service and, anyway, Donal was born in 1940. She did everything for us.

She and daddy both felt guilty about Aileen who, God bless her, was at the very least bipolar and probably suffered from undiagnosed Asperger's. Guilty, though nothing that was wrong with Aileen's life was their fault. They did everything they could for her.

Mammy would slave over Christmas dinner – the turkey would hang in the larder for a few days before the Big Day. I'd get to eat the gizzard and the rest of the innards!

She was, in many ways, the boss.

'Daddy, can we go to the pictures?'

'Ask your mother.'

'Mammy, daddy says it's okay to go to the pictures if you say it's okay.' It invariably was.

Mammy had no idea daddy was dying. She was too close and probably in denial. But she was devastated. Alone after all those years together. We all visited mammy a lot though I think she was lonely in her apartment. One time, years later, when I visited her in Dalkey in Our Lady's Manor, she told me she had begun praying to her parents.

'Why?' I asked.

'They got me into this...' she said, in fairness, smiling.

She cried the few times she spoke to me about her father who died when she was five. She mentioned her mother only once to me, saying that after her father was killed (he went missing) in the First World War every time there was a knock on the door, she thought it was him. She always hoped he had lost his memory or had been taken prisoner.

My granny – her name was Lily – was the first braille teacher in Ireland and also 'Mother Macree', the 'agony aunt', in a Catholic magazine. She died when my mum was 14, I think.

Mum was close to her sister Una and, after her brother Gerard, a commandant in the army, died in a car crash in the late 1950s, she remained in close contact with her sister-in-law Emer.

Now? In my mind's eye I see mammy in bed in the morning and me bending down to give her a kiss before going to school. I see her walking beside me into Clarendon Street Church. I see her talking with a neighbour, or welcoming her bridge playing friends, Máire, Maura and Marie, on a Wednesday afternoon. I see her in the garden tending her beloved plants. I see her across the table in the Montrose Hotel where we went once a week for lunch. I see her in her bed in Our Lady's Manor, no longer able to leave it. She was a wonderful mother.

They were wonderful parents. I love them as much today as ever. And I know they're together in heaven with Aileen.

Lallser

I mentioned my sister Aileen before. She died in December 2012 after a life struggling with Bipolar disease and, we are pretty sure, Asperger's. I remember twice when Aileen took me, as a young lad, for what were unforgettable experiences.

The first was to Butlins in Mosney. We were there for a week. And while I loved swimming and playing in the Scalextric room and going on the carnival rides and what not, Aileen patiently indulged the ten-year-old me. The only thing I remember doing together was going out in a rowing boat on the lake. And, if I remember correctly, she wasn't happy until we were on dry land again.

But another time, she took me to the National Stadium to hear Handel's *Hallelujah Chorus* being performed. And that too was unforgettable. Just as Aileen is.

She had a tough life. She never settled in any school despite being very bright. But her psychiatric problems, manic depression (bipolar they call it now), surfaced and caused no end of worry for my parents who fretted more about Aileen than any of us. Daddy called her Lallser Lou.

Aileen was in and out of St John of Gods, but still managed to be a brilliant nurse in the Army. We think now that she probably had Asperger's because she had zero social skills. Her one-time best friend told me at her funeral that Aileen was the best friend you could have 'until she got sick' at the end of her teens. Aileen had a child, having been used and abused by some bastard who further ruined what was already a difficult life. And he took her money as well. We don't know who or where he is and don't want to know.

After her funeral one of my brothers asked the other:

'Do you think Aileen ever went home, once in her life, and said, "that was a great day?"'

And after thinking about it for a second, the answer was: 'No.'

I hope she's happy now in heaven with mammy and daddy.

My Father and the Famine

Here's an amazing thing. My father was born in 1913 in Templederry, near Nenagh in Tipperary, and died in 1978. But only recently my brother Donal told me that dad once said that he had met a man who described the Great Famine – because he had lived through it!

The Great Famine was from 1845 to 1852. So let's assume by the time my dad heard this story he was ten, say in 1923. The famine ended in 1852, 71 years earlier, so a man of, say, 81, would have been ten at the time and would, surely, have vivid memories of such a traumatic period. I find that astonishing.

It brought to mind the story of a headline that once appeared in an Irish newspaper at some point in the twentieth century. The headline read: I met a man who met a man who met Napper Tandy.

The famine, to me, was so long ago as to be 'ancient' history. But it wasn't. I am the son of a man who knew someone who lived through the famine.

Christmas

It would begin as soon as we came home from Mass. My five siblings and I would rush into the living room as soon as our father unlocked the door. There, we would find what Santa had brought for us, a small pile for each, labelled, and on a chair. An empty glass and a few crumbs on a plate where I, as the youngest, would have left milk and a slice of cake for the great man. It was a routine I enjoyed until I was 12. As the oldest, my brother enjoyed it until he was 26. Such is life.

We would barely have the wrapping off the toys when we would smell the bacon cooking. It was the start of a long, long day of eating, eating and more eating. We would sit down for the fry-up, rashers, sausages, eggs, black and white pudding, tomatoes, toast and tea. And when it was eaten, some of us did the washing up and some managed to avoid doing it.

Sometimes, during the morning, a neighbour might call and the kettle would go on and scones or buns or some such would be offered around with cups of tea.

Before long, it was time for elevenses. We didn't always have elevenses in our house. But on Christmas day, we did. More tea. More food. More ritual stuffing of the face. And then, the build up to our Christmas dinner – at lunchtime.

Those who had left home and were married would arrive shortly before the appointed time. My grand aunt and uncle would be shown to seats in the living room and be offered a cup of tea which, before they had time to drink it, would be abandoned in favour of the main event.

Dinner. The full whack. Starter, soup, turkey and ham and God knows how many vegetables and mashed spuds and roast spuds and gravy and cranberry sauce and, of course, wine for the older ones and lots of Club Orange and Club Lemon for the younger ones and the Pioneers, of whom there were many, and then fruit salad and trifle and plum pudding which never seemed to light properly and coffee and tea and the washing up. For some of us. Others again managed to avoid doing it.

When all was washed and dried and put away, my father and his brother would sit back and snooze for a little while.

It mattered not that, in the early years, toy trains, brought by Santa, might be making noise or children might be whinging over the lack of batteries in an age when nothing, not a thing, opened on Christmas day.

The two of them slept. And when they awoke, my father would read out the labels on the gifts which had been piled under the tree. 'From Donal to Úna,' he would say and I'd hand the wrapped gift to Úna. 'From John to Mammy,' he'd say and I'd give the gift to my mother. On it went. 'From Donal to Diarmuid, from Aileen to Patrick, from Diarmuid to Auntie Kathleen, from Aileen to Uncle Paddy...' Until they were all distributed.

When all the presents had been doled out, my mother would ask if anyone wanted tea. And in would come the tray with tea and biscuits and Christmas cake. And we'd drink tea and eat. Again. And some of us would wash up again and some would avoid it.

But when the washing up was done, there was barely time to see the end of the circus or whatever it was they were showing on RTÉ that afternoon before we'd be invited back into the dining room for tea. Tea was, well, tea and turkey sandwiches and ham sandwiches and cake and cheese and grapes. And we'd all eat again and drink again and some of us would wash up again and some would avoid it again.

And then we'd watch RTÉ's variety show or BBC's variety show or ITV's variety show. Because they all had their own variety shows, at least until Morecambe and Wise took over at Christmas with theirs. And like all the variety shows of the time, they'd have Bruce Forsyth on or Val Doonican or Vince Hill or Matt Monro or Shirley Bassey.

And when it was over, and we were all tired and full and ready to call it a day and my Uncle and Grand Aunt had gone, my mother would look up from the television. And she'd ask the question. The inevitable question. Would anyone like a cup of tea or a sandwich?

Christmas Day 1978 was difficult. My father had died on November 29 that year and he and my mother were very much the centre of our Christmases. Our mum – we were too old to call her mammy by now – prepared the meal and was at it for days in advance. The turkey was hung, plucked and gutted and she made sure everything was absolutely spot on.

But the presents? Well, they were all put into black sacks, labeled with the recipient's name and handed out. The announcing of giver and receiver was a tradition which died with my father.

The Fuse

As I have mentioned before, my father was Chairman and Chief Executive of the ESB. He and Mammy didn't hold too many dinner parties – bridge parties, yes – but only a few dinner parties as I remember. One such was on New Year's Eve in about 1968 or so.

As my mother worked her miracles in the kitchen, the older children (all bar me) were getting ready to go out for the night. Every light in the house was on. Hairdryers were going. The heating was on. The cooker (electric of course) was going full blast. The television was on.

Then the first guest arrived and pressed the doorbell. And that was it. The system could take no more. It shut down. The main fuse blew.

In those days that wasn't a thing you could fix yourself. It required the experts from the ESB, and remember, it was 8.00 or so on New Year's Eve. I think it was Dee who made the call.

'Our main fuse is gone,' he said. 'Could you get someone around to fix it as soon as possible?'

I'm not sure if there was a snigger at the other end of the line or not. But the reply was along the lines of it not being possible, it was New Year's Eve and it might be a day or two before anyone could get there.

'What's the name and address?'

'It's Tom Murray on Sycamore Road, Mount Merrion.'

A pause at the other end.

'Murray? Sycamore Road?'

'Yes,' Dee said.

'We'll be there in five mintues.' And they were.

No strings were pulled, no mention was made of who lived in the house. But they knew.

The Minister

There were many strikes in the ESB in the early days of my father's tenure as chairman there. On one occasion, in the middle of a strike, we took a phone call at home in Mount Merrion from the then Minister for Transport and Power Erskine Childers. The minister was informed that my father was out but was expected home shortly. He said he'd call later. My father came home and was given the message.

About ten minutes later, the doorbell rang, I answered. It was the Minister. When he said he'd call later, he meant call to the house. My mother showed him into the living room and closed the door so that he and my father could have a private discussion.

But they hadn't reckoned with my Auntie Emer who was with us for the day. She stood in the hall and, in a very posh voice, started saying things like:

'Ask the butler to go to the west wing and bring the wine back', and, 'Has the chef not prepared lunch for us – we're all in the dining room.' And so on.

We laughed. She was having so much fun, and so were we, that nobody tried to stop her. What the minister made of her we don't know. He never said. Thank God.

Girlfriends

I think I fancied Leslie when I was eight or so down in Rosslare. I know I fancied Saibh when I was the Irish College in Ring in 1964. Sadly, she fancied a lad named Billy. Dara was my first proper girlfriend. I think that ended because I was boarding in Blackrock College in Sixth Year.

In college, I was crazy about Annie but it wasn't reciprocated (are you beginning to see a pattern here?). We were great friends in college and did loads together. But on one side there was like, and on the other, a bit more. Infatuation maybe. But I was much too serious. Still think she was great.

I fell in love with Paula Parkinson at work in the *Indo* and we married in 1975 when I was 21 and she just 18. My father said to us: 'You're far too young but I wish you all the best.' Lack of maturity was the problem, mine mostly. We lasted almost 15 years and I still have nothing but respect for Paula.

Connie Clinton. Work again. I fell in love with Connie as my marriage was teetering, probably because of my immaturity. She's wonderful and brave and extraordinary. Connie was Sport Editor of the *Star*, not just the first female sports editor probably anywhere but certainly in Ireland, but was voted Sports Editors' Sports Editor by her peers. She survived two brain haemorrhages; the first one in 1999 was almost fatal. And she gave me Charlotte, the last girl in my life and the one who I love more than life.

The Scouts

My brother John was in the scouts in Blackrock College. The 77th Troop. Why he was the first brother to join, I don't know, but I followed him. Even now, 50 years later, I'd recommend the scouts to anyone. Mighty craic. And a bit of growing up.

At the start, of course, you just do what you're told, often by someone not much older than you. I was in the Lions Patrol as far as I remember. Mostly, scouting consisted of tying knots and earning merit badges and hikes to Powerscourt and, well, Powerscourt. We occasionally went to Larch Hill for a night. But it was in summer that our scouting really became fun.

I remember the year we camped in Carrog, North Wales, on the banks of the River Dee. It was great fun. Until it started raining. And raining. And raining. In fact, it rained so much that we could see the river rising, quickly, to the level of the field in which we were camped. So we decamped to a church hall and spent the rest of the week there.

We attended a jamboree in Lismore, in the grounds of the Castle. Thousands of us (well, it could have been hundreds but it felt like thousands). Scouts from all over the world together for a week.

The big one, though, was our continental trip when I was 14 or 15. All in for £50. (My mother later explained that it was £50 plus five times that spent on cakes, raffle tickets, rubbish at sales and what not.) We flew to London, from there to Munich where we spent a few days before heading to Innsbruck and then on a train to La Spezia in Italy.

We didn't know that continental trains split every now and then with carriages going off in different directions, and so, instead of La Spezia, four of us ended up in Rimini. Another four ended up in Rome. But, by some miracle and not a little skill on the part of our scoutmasters, we all made it to La Spezia in the end. Remember, this was 30 years or more before mobile phones arrived on the scene.

We left La Spezia a day early because a couple of us had made friends with two girls, Nellie and Roberta. The scout master wasn't pleased and we were all packed onto the train and we ended up in Grenoble. So rushed was our exit from La Spezia that we arrived in Grenoble late at night and had no way of getting to our campsite. So we bedded down in the station much to the displeasure of the officials there.

They then announced that, as the last train had arrived and there were no more departures, they were closing the station. So we were thrown out. As soon as the doors closed, they opened again and we went to go in.

'Sorry,' they said, 'unless you have a valid ticket for travel, you can't come in.'

So we slept outside which wasn't a hardship. Indeed, on another night, we chose to sleep outside and look at the Perseid meteor shower which, because we were so far south, was magnificent. We made it home and I was broke as ever having spent all my money in the first week of our two week trip.

I stayed a scout for a few of my teenage years until, well, girls and discos and music took over. But I've no regrets at all. None. A fantastic organisation. And my daughter now is enjoying the scouts as much as I ever did.

The Weddings

As mentioned, I married twice. In 1975, at just 21, I married Paula Parkinson who was just 18. We married in the church in Kilbarrack, Paula's parish, and had a lovely, small reception in Clontarf Castle. Beamish was my only friend present. I couldn't afford to invite any more. In fact, I couldn't afford the reception at all.

As we were wrapping up the day – Paula and I were heading back to England a few days later – I was given the bill. It was well over a grand. And we're talking 1973. It might as well have been millions. I hadn't a snowball's chance of paying it. My father stood beside me.

'Show me,' he said.

I showed him.

'I'll look after that,' he said.

You already know how wonderful I think he was. But that was just extraordinary.

My second wedding was in 2008. In fairness, once Connie had given birth to Charlotte, Paula agreed to a divorce. So I put that in motion. A date in early December 2008, I think it was the ninth, was arranged for the court and the divorce. And then I called the registrar to arrange a date for the wedding.

'I can't even meet you to discuss it until July I'm so busy,' I was told, 'unless you can do it on December 12, I've had a cancellation.'

So we did. Divorced on the ninth and married on the twelfth, having first met in early 1990. And lovely it was with just my family. The music was 'World in Union' (the rugby world cup theme) and 'Fix You' by Coldplay. And when we got home, our friends Michael and Brenda Croke had organised a red carpet for the path to our front door with a violinist inside playing beautiful music. We had a lovely meal with our families. And here we still are....

Life at UCD

Starting Third Level

Going to UCD wasn't my idea. In fact, apart from doing absolutely nothing other than hanging around the place, very little was my idea. But despite pretty poor results in the Leaving Cert I somehow got into First Commerce in UCD, which was a bit like putting someone who only spoke Swahili into the English faculty. You see, I got a D in Pass Maths in the Leaving Cert and I went straight from that into the Commerce Department in UCD. First lecture was Logic.

'Ah here,' I thought, having struggled with long division.

Day one, Professor Quigley marched to the podium and began to talk about logic. He lost me the minute he opened his mouth. The result was that I didn't attend many more lectures that year. Six in total.

Comedy

But it was a good year socially and in relation to all things comedic. Comedy and Annie.

I am proud to say that I did not come last in First Commerce, though a glance at the marks I achieved would suggest that I tried hard to gain that distinction: Economics 25, Maths 15, Accountancy....well, okay, zero.

I moved on to Journalism in Rathmines where the wonderful Louis McRedmond was our main teacher. And I was home!

Michael Collins' Chair

I was deeply involved with UCD's Commerce and Economics Society – the C&E – during my year in college, 1971/72, and for two subsequent years. That resulted in a friendship with Beamish, Brendan Martin, which has lasted until this day. We had many guests at the C&E, but one night we had the British Labour politician Merlyn Rees – later Northern Ireland secretary – and his Conservative counterpart William 'Bill' Deedes. It was a good night at the society.

When the debate was over, the committee and our two guests adjourned to Newman House on Stephen's Green where we were guests of UCD Chaplain Fr Paul Spellman. It was awkward. It seemed the two men weren't mad about each other. The conversation between our small group – there were only five or six in the room – was stifled.

Fr Spellman broke the ice. He pointed to a chair, an antique looking carver, and announced that it had been Michael Collins' chair. Well, the two British politicians were fascinated. They took turns sitting in it. They talked not just to us but to each other about Ireland and Collins and history. Then the calls, separate calls, came to tell them their cars were there to bring them to the airport for their flights home. We all shook hands and they left.

So we wandered over to look at the chair, as fascinated as our British guests had been. 'So this was Michael Collins chair?' I said, thinking out loud…

'Not at all,' said Fr Spellman. 'But I had to say something to break the ice.'

I presume he confessed his lie the following day.

The Machine

Once I realised that Commerce wasn't for me I had to find something else to occupy my mind for the year. I managed to hook up with Brendan Martin (Beamish), Billy McGrath, Brian McCormack (Stopper) and Kevin Kiely. For reasons that are quite complicated, we morphed into a comedy group called the Spike Milligan Election Machine, later shortened to just

The Machine. (Oh very well. We launched a campaign to have Spike made an honorary Vice President of the Commerce and Economics Society and we were his Election Machine. He was. He accepted. And we went on from there.)

The five became three – Beamish, Billy and I – and for a couple of years, we put on shows in the massive Theatre L in UCD in Belfield. Mad stuff. Wacky stuff. Monty Pythonesque. In fairness, we filled the place.

I remember one person, who later became a friend, coming to us one day offering a sketch he had written. It was Dermot Morgan. He formed his own troupe, Big Gom and the Imbeciles, and of course went on to great heights with Father Ted.

Our shows were fun. The students loved them. They were events. In fact, in one way or another, we all kept in touch with the entertainment world. Billy went on to be an RTÉ, then independent, television producer; Beamish went on to work for two television magazines, the *RTÉ Guide* and then *Radio Times*, and at various stages we all wrote comedy.

Beamish and I managed to secure a meeting with David Hatch who eventually became head of light entertainment on BBC Radio. I can't imagine such a thing happening now. But David met us in his office at Aeolian Hall in London. He asked if we wanted to be writers or performers. Before Beamish could say 'all three' I, apparently, blurted out 'writers'. As we had agreed not to argue in front of him, Beamish said nothing. Until afterwards!

So we had work accepted for BBC Radio Four's satirical programme, *Weekending*, which was produced by John Lloyd, who went on to make *Spitting Image, Blackadder* and *QI* amongst other things. And it starred David Jason, who went on to make *Open All Hours* and *Only Fools and Horses* amongst others. We also wrote for Dave Allen, who became huge, and the Two Ronnies – what can I say about them other than we wrote hundreds of lines for them and they used two.

You might also find my name, and maybe the other lads' names as well, on the credits for the *Live Mike*, *The Late Late Show*, *The Saturday Night Show with Brendan O'Connor*, and shows with Oliver Callan and Brendan Grace, among others.

Sniffer Magee

And of course I have to mention the *Twink Show*. That show is famous for a number of things. Firstly, it was, of course, where Twink's cleaning lady character, who had a big impact at the Fine Gael Ard Fheis, first appeared. Secondly, it was where John McColgan and Moya Doherty first met – and they went on to become probably the most successful couple in Irish entertainment history with *Riverdance*. And thirdly, there was Sniffer Magee. Who?

Well, one of the characters Twink played in what was a pretty sharp programme was a pirate radio DJ called Cynthia Brewster St James. And one day she played a request for Sniffer Magee from Finglas.

'No,' John said. 'No more Sniffer Magee.'

I had invented Sniffer Magee, but John killed him off. And guess which one of us went on to become a millionaire?

Debating and Adrian Hardiman

I loved debating, winning a gold medal for it at the C&E one year. I had a chance to win gold too at the famous L&H, but on the final night of the year, when an impromptu debate was held to decide the winner, the then Auditor Adrian Hardiman asked me to pull out.

'Even if you won tonight, you're too far behind to win the medal,' he said.

I believed him. But it was a lie!

We didn't fall out over it. When it came to the machinations of UCD societies, we were too similar. Indeed, we conspired once or twice to have a go at some of those in college to whom we were both opposed.

We didn't meet again for years as I went off to be a hack and he rose to the heights of the Supreme Court.

Then, in March 2016, I was beside Adrian when he died. I was in St James' Hospital A&E department having arrived by ambulance with a heart problem. Adrian was wheeled into the next cubicle and I could hear the doctors fight to save him.

I survived. He didn't. It was just the most extraordinary and tragic of moments.

No Standing Upstarts

It wasn't long after the writer Ulick O'Connor had appeared in court charged with assaulting a bus conductor that he was a guest speaker at the L&H. As he stood to speak he didn't know that someone (not me) had a little plan. Before he could open his mouth, the first student stood.

'Fares, please, fares please, ding ding ding,' he said in a Dublin accent, mimicking the voice of a bus conductor and the sound of the bell on his ticket machine.

Our old friend, the muffled titter, ran around the room. Ulick almost smiled. Sixty seconds elapsed. Ulick opened his mouth to speak. On the far side of the theatre, a second student stood.

'Move along the car now please, move along the car. Ding ding.'

The muffled titter went for another run. Ulick's smile narrowed. He opened his mouth. Only 15 seconds had passed since the last 'conductor' when yet another stood.

'Plenty of room on top now, ding ding, plenty of room upstairs.'

Ulick grimaced. Another student stood.

'No standing up stairs now please, ding ding.'

Then another.

'Fares please, anyone lookin' for a ticket?'

And three more.

'Anyone need a ticket? Ding ding.'

'Move along now please, move along.'

'Fare please, fares please.'

Soon, 12 students were standing and shouting bus conductor-type things. Then 15. Then 20. And Ulick gave up.

The muffled titter had become uproarious laughter. And I'm pretty sure I saw at least three men who eventually became judges – one in the Supreme Court – another who became a well known broadcaster, several soon to be business leaders, a future senior politician and, maybe, a future journalist and writer of a blog among the 'bus conductors'.

No names, of course.

The Hippy

Ubi Dwyer was a famous eccentric and hippy. Indeed, in 1971, he visited Dornish Island in Clew Bay which had been bought some years previously by John Lennon and which was later occupied by Sid Rawle, King of the Hippies. It wasn't the only hippy commune in Ireland.

For a time Bill Ubi Dwyer and a few other assorted anarchists lived in a kind of commune on the site of what is now the Merrion Shopping Centre. I was often bunking off school and some days I spent planting potatoes with Ubi and his friends at the commune which they called The Island. Bonkers stuff really for a 16-year-old, but a bit of an adventure. And another example of my utter and complete irresponsibility, something for which I had become known in school. And, sadly, at home.

Summer Jobs in London, 1972

As mentioned earlier, I headed for London in the summer of 1972. The plan was to earn money for college the following September. Well, that's what I said the plan was. I knew I had done so badly in my first year that a second was unlikely. So the real plan was to have fun.

No Thanks

The first job I had was in the Shell Centre on the river. I was a cleaner in the chauffeurs' garage. It was a great job because the chauffeurs' garage was never other than spotless. Happy days. Well, until some supervisor or other came up and told us there was a little job in Barclay's Bank which was in the basement of the building. It was a job which for which he had, essentially, volunteered us.

Down we went. He explained that they had a problem with their sewage works and that the toilets had, basically, coughed back what had gone into them. The floor was a foot deep in, not to put to fine a point on it, shit. He handed me and the other guy hand brushes and dust pans.

'You can put the soiled tissue in the bins,' he said.

'Excuse me,' I said, and I promise this is out of character and was prompted by his arrogance and presumption that we would do what he instructed. 'I come from a very wealthy family,' I lied, 'and I am here only as part of a social experiment to see how people like you live. I have seen enough. Good day.'

No. I wasn't very pleasant to him. But I wasn't picking up other people's shit either. So I handed him my rubber gloves.

The Crown and Two Chairmen

Next, I went to an agency and they got me fixed up as a barman because of my (coughs) experience. It was in a wonderful place called The Crown and Two Chairmen on Dean Street in Soho. I was happy there for three weeks and then I was fired. I couldn't figure it out. I had done nothing wrong. It was later that I discovered that the fee payable to the agency which had sent me there only became due if I stayed longer than three weeks.

The pub was next door to a club called The Sunset Strip. The girls, the strippers, used to drink in the Crown and Two Chairmen. They were actually very nice girls. They took their clothes off for a living but had a very strict 'thus far and no further' rule in place.

I became friendly with some of them. Indeed, I spent part of my nineteenth birthday in Soho Square with a stripper called Annie and one of the other girls from the Sunset Strip, along with my old school friend Michael Ducie, drinking champagne out of plastic cups. If my mother and father had known...

The Sunset Strip

Anyway, when they heard I had been fired, they got me temporary work in the Sunset Strip, sweeping up back stage and that kind of thing. It was only for a week or so but it paid the (drinks) bill.

De Hems

Then I moved to De Hems, a pub off Shaftsbury Avenue. It was okay. One day there was a large gang in for lunch. Men in suits, dolly birds and so on. When they'd finished, they got up and were walking out without paying. I tried to stop them. The manager almost had a fit.

'No,' he whispered loudly. 'They don't pay.'

Gangsters. So I moved on.

Cockney Pride Tavern

Next was the Cockney Pride Tavern on Piccadilly. The man who hired us, a Scottish man who had retired from Scotland Yard, didn't like Irish people. 'Thieving Irish c**ts,' he called us. 'If I could find anyone else to hire I would but I'm stuck with you thieving Irish *****.'

Now, I never took as much as a penny anywhere I worked. But, well…

Anyway, on Friday when I was due to collect my £17 wages, he called me down and accused me of stealing. He said the assistant manager was watching us. I told him we knew because the assistant manager wasn't exactly subtle. He searched me. And then told me to fuck off out of the place, he wasn't paying me.

I walked out. I walked three, maybe four streets and if he had seen me, he might have seen a bead of sweat or two running down my forehead. When I was far enough away, I reached into my tie and took out the fiver I had stuffed there. I had stuffed one there every night of the six I worked in the place – £30 instead of £17. He deserved it. Anyway, I was out of work again.

Great American Disaster

I found work in the Great American Disaster on Fulham Road, a trendy hamburger joint. I was the busboy, bringing dishes to the kitchen and clearing tables and so on. It was brilliant. I loved it. And some of the waiters shared their tips. The only problem was I had to move from my brother's place in Kingsbury into Cromwell Road where, I think, about 12 of us shared a two bedroomed flat. It wasn't so bad. Those of us who worked in catering of some sort didn't get into bed until the early hours because that's when the builders were getting out of the beds. Worked like a dream.

That was the last job. The call to go to journalism college came and I went home. Penniless. Total amount saved towards college? £0 Amount borrowed (!) from father to get home by train and boat? €30.

My old job? Well, a friend called Dave asked me not to give notice. He said he'd take over. He turned up the following Monday and told the manager he was me, or not exactly me, but that I had given him the job. The manager, a decent man from Kildare, smiled and said, 'Did he indeed?' But he hired him.

A Tired Girl

It would be wrong to leave that London episode without telling the story of our friend – I won't name him just in case – who worked with us in the Cockney Pride Tavern. It wasn't a great place to work, to be honest, but it was a job. Two or three of us worked there behind one of the bars. And there was waitress service too.

One of those waitresses was from Sweden. And I know how clichéd that sounds but she was. And every day, she'd arrive into the pub wearing a coat. She would go straight to the girls' changing rooms where, we were told, she would remove her coat under which she wore just her underwear, before changing into her waitress's uniform. The lads all fancied her.

And then, one night, one of the guys who shared our apartment told us that this girl had asked him to walk her home. We were astonished. He was the least likely for her to fancy. But that's life.

We got home and spoke of little else. (We had to stay up until about 5.00 until the builders got out of the beds so we could get into them.)

We thought our friend wouldn't be home. But about an hour after we got home, he arrived. We couldn't wait for the story.

'What happened?' we asked as one.

'Well, I walked her to her flat. And when we got in, she took off her coat...'

Our jaws dropped.

'And then she said she wanted to go to bed. So I told her I was knackered myself and came home.'

'What?!'

We didn't know whether to laugh or cry. A beautiful Swedish girl had stood in front of him wearing nothing but her underwear and told him she wanted to go to bed.

And he came home. Fifty years later, it's still hard to credit.

To be fair I'll fess up to something I did which was similar. It was towards the end of the summer and I was in the house my brother was sharing with a few other Irish lads. The phone rang. Whoever answered turned to me and said:

'It's Annie for you.'

'Tell her I've had to go back to Ireland urgently,' I said. He did. And hung up.

Then he asked me: 'Who's Annie?'

'Oh,' I said, 'she's one of the girls from Sunset Strip. They're having a party at the weekend and wanted me to come along. I didn't fancy it.'

There was a short silence. And then I think the words which followed were:

'You stupid little bollix.'

Further Childhood Adventures

Minerva

English was probably the only subject I really enjoyed in school. Come the Leaving Cert, despite doing little or no work, I managed to achieve honours, largely because the three poets I liked and had studied – Yeats, Kavanagh and Emily Dickinson – suited the three poetry questions asked.

That summer, I helped publish a poetry magazine. We called it *Minerva*. And I remember David Kane and Peter Finley working on it. We managed to persuade Peter Fallon to contribute – and he was just about the hippest poet around at the time. John McManus designed the cover. We got £50 from the Arts Council to pay for it to be printed. It sold in the Eblana Bookshop on Grafton Street and I think we sold more than 100 in total. I can't find my copy now – but I checked, and there is one in the National Library.

Dogs

I remember five dogs in my life. My sister Úna had Jessie, a Springer Spaniel and, like all lovable dogs, quite mad. Jessie actually smiled.

In another part of my life, my former wife Paula got Ruffles, a lovable mongrel, for her mother. He was wonderful. And I remember vividly the day he had to be put to sleep how he looked at me from the vet's table as if to say thanks, before the lethal injection was administered.

Then there was Lucy, another little mongrel we had in Sandymount. An adorable little thing who lived to a ripe old age.

Eric was probably my favourite. He was a Samoyed Connie got me for my fiftieth birthday. Not only did we love him, everyone who every saw him loved him. When we went walking all sorts of people, especially children, wanted to come over and say hello to Eric. He walked with swaying back legs like I've never seen on another dog.

One day we knew he wasn't in great form – I had taken him out for a walk and he didn't bother running around the park. Then he lay in his spot in the living room and didn't re-act when we mentioned that it was Charlotte's bedtime which normally brought a few barks. He stopped moving and our neighbour, Danny, helped carry him to the car. I brought him to the emergency vet in UCD but he was already dead. We kept his ashes.

Now, we have Penny. We got Penny from Connie's broth-er-in-law Benny shortly after his wife and Connie's sister Mary died. Penny is a noisy dote who barks her head off any time anyone passes the house. But we love her anyway.

Murder

My daughter Charlotte thinks I am a murderer. And there is some justification for that. I did kill something. But it was an accident. I had actually tried to be kind to Joey. Joey, the victim.

Joey was found dead one morning, lying on his back with his legs in the air. And I was the one who had killed him.

Joey, you see, was a budgie. And I was about five years of age. What happened was this.

Each night, we covered Joey's cage so that he would sleep or do whatever it is budgies do at night. But just after the cover had been put on, I decided to share with Joey the sweets I had been given that day – big, pink, soft marshmallows.

So I shoved one into his cage and thought very highly of myself for having shared my sweets. Unfortunately, Joey liked the idea of eating a marshmallow. He stuck his beak in to taste a little bit of it and it became stuck fast. This, of course, prevented the little thing from breathing and so...

Well, when the cover was lifted the next morning, poor Joey was on his back, legs in the air, marshmallow still stuck to his beak. It was, at worst, manslaughter, or budgieslaughter. Doesn't stop Charlotte from rejoicing in telling people: My dad murdered a budgie.

The Big Spoof

I have been known, occasionally, to spoof a little. Back in the 1960s, when I was in the Blackrock College Scout Troop, the 44th, we had a soccer team. One day, based on absolutely nothing except some fantasy in my mind, I said I'd be able to organise a match against St Patrick's Athletic. Pats are, of course, a League of Ireland team and I had no connection with them whatsoever, high up or low down. I suppose I hoped I'd be ignored.

But no. 'Organise a game then,' I was told.

Pats' manager at the time was John Colrain, a former Celtic player. So I wrote to him. Lo and behold, he wrote back and said we could have a game against their youth team. We did. I had to miss it. (Knowing me, I more than likely funked it.) We were beaten but the lads had enjoyed it.

I wrote to *Shoot!* Magazine to tell them how good John had been to us. A week or so later, John, who died very young at 47, called me one evening to thank me. A real gentleman. Who else would call a kid, a teenager, to thank him when it was John who did me the favour? Class.

Buoyed by my success, I told my scout buddies I'd get them a match against Shamrock Rovers. Rovers were then the best team in Ireland. They are still and will probably always be the best known. Well, I wrote to the club and of course they

181

wrote back saying they'd be delighted to play us but we'd have to provide the venue.

This time I did play. The game was played in St Michael's College grounds on Ailesbury Road in Ballsbridge. I'd bet it was the first soccer game ever played on that particular road. Rovers beat us 3-0 which wasn't bad bearing in mind their experience compared to ours.

My spoofing was gathering momentum. So I said we'd get a game against Manchester United. I think skepticism best describes the response. At the back of it all, I suspect they knew I'd been spoofing about Pats and Rovers but just got lucky.

'Go on then.' The challenge was issued.

I wrote to Manchester United's secretary Les Olive. Guess what? He wrote back and said that of course they'd love to play us. In Manchester!

So we organised it. We picked a date, I cleared it with Les, I mean, Mr Olive. And early in January we got the boat to Liverpool, slept there in a scout hall for the night and went on to The Cliff, United's training ground for the game.

Okay, it didn't turn out to be what you'd call the most competitive game in history. The ground was covered in snow. But then, it was covered in snow for both of us. Mind you, their footwear was a little bit more suitable than ours. We had studs. They didn't. Mind you, they also had class and we didn't. We played their youth team or Under 16s or something.

It was five nil at half time. Or was it six. Could have been seven. For *them* of course. So we mixed the teams. Well, their coach mixed the teams a) to let them get some practice and b) to stop further humiliation.

And when it was over, their coach – couldn't tell you who it was and we were too overawed to get the names of the United players we faced – said he was really impressed by one of our players. Our goalkeeper, Richie O'Connor! He let in a bag-ful and he was our best player! Well, okay, he couldn't stop the bagful because the defence, of which I was part, was useless against the class of the United players.

Still, we had fun. And when it was all over, we had played Pats, Rovers and United. I hadn't the nerve to mention Real Madrid...

But there you are. Three spoofs. And they all turned out not to be spoofs at all!

The Pencil

I presume you are familiar with those pencils which have, on the top, a little eraser. There is a small, cylindrical piece of rubber, encased in a bit of tin, on the top of the pencil. Try to visualise this. I am about six years of age and doing my homework. I have, in my hand, one of the above described pencils. In this case, the rubber is either worn or chewed away.

So all there is at the top of the pencil is a bit of relatively sharp tin. And I'm resting it on my front teeth as I think, presumably about the homework. Or maybe ice cream. And then it slips.

It slips from my tooth and runs along the roof of my mouth, scraping and tearing away the skin as it does. I run to my mother. Blood is pouring from my mouth. She looks in and sees a piece of skin hanging down. She picks me up. I'm a sturdy six year old and my mother is not much more than five feet tall and fifty years old. She carries me out our front door and up Trees Road half a mile or more uphill, all the time time I'm in her arms, crying and bleeding.

We finally get to Dr Spellman's house and he lets us in. Those were the days when you could call to your GP in an emergency. Dr Spellman was concerned. He sits me down. My mother is out of breath and jaded. Dr Spellman looks into my mouth. He sees the piece of skin hanging down. He picks up a pair of scissors. He holds my mouth open and puts the scissors in. He cuts away the piece of hanging skin.

'Grand,' he says or something along those lines. 'He'll be okay in the morning.'

And I was.

The Future Lawyer

It was obvious from a very early age that my brother Dee would study law. And if it wasn't obvious before the chocolate cake incident, it was afterwards.

I was about nine and Dee was maybe 14 or so. My mother put a piece of chocolate cake on the table and told us we could share it. Dee cut the cake. One slice was two-thirds, the other one-third. He gave me the small piece.

'Hey,' I said. 'That's greedy.'

'What's greedy?' he asked.

'You cut the cake and you took the big bit,' I said.

'What would you have done?' he asked me.

'I would have taken the small bit,' I said.

His response?

'Well, you have it.'

Fancy Dress

I once wore my sister Una's wedding dress to a fancy dress party.

I thought it was funny. She didn't.

PART 3 – MORE FROM THE MIDDLE . . .

Six Degrees of Separation

In Australia

I was in Australia reporting on Gay Byrne's adventures there. And I had arranged to meet someone in the Irish Club in Sydney. I got there early and waited. But the person I was supposed to meet hadn't turned up half an hour after the appointed time and I had to be somewhere else.

So I approached the elderly barman and asked if I could leave a note for my contact. He said I could. As I wrote, I asked him where he was from.

'Tipperary,' he said. And he told me he hadn't been 'home' for 40 years or more.

I told him my father was from Tipperary. And as I handed him the note, which I had signed, he asked me where in Tipperary my father was from.

'Templederry,' I said.

He looked at the note.

'You'd be Tom's son,' he said.

I was astonished.

'How do you know?'

'Well, you're from Dublin. So you're not John or Dan's. Paddy is a priest so that leaves Jim and Tom. And Jim's in Kildare, so I reckoned it had to be Tom.'

I stood with my mouth open, amazed at this man's recollection of a place and people he had left almost half a century before. Sadly, I no longer recall his name. But he made that particular day for me.

In South Africa

I was in South Africa for the Rugby World Cup in 1995 and when we got to Capetown, I linked up with Mick Mackey. We decided that we would take the cable car up Table Mountain on day one because we knew that if we spent a couple of days looking up at what was then a rickety cable car, we wouldn't do it. So we got to the top where there was a nice, outdoor, area in which we could have a beer. The waiter arrived over.

'Can I get ye a drink lads?' he said with his Irish accent.

'Where are you from?' I asked him.

'Nenagh,' he said.

'Do you know Eileen Scroope?' I asked him.

'She taught me in school,' he said.

'She's my auntie,' I said. 'Two Coors Light.'

In the Same Band

Charlotte was on a play day in her friend Marianne McHugh's house. I went to pick her up and Marianne's dad, Kevin, let me in. The girls were still playing, so we went in to the living room and sat down. I sat on the couch and there was a guitar beside me. I absent mindedly picked it up and started strumming.

'Do you play?' Kevin asked me.

'Not really,' I said. 'I was in a band when I was a teenager.'

'Was that in Terenure?' Kevin asked me.

'No. I'm from Mount Merrion. That's where the band was from,' I said.

'I had a cousin living in Mount Merrion,' Kevin said.

'What was his name?' I asked.

'Neil McHugh,' Kevin said.

'He was in the band too,' I said as the remaining hair on the back of my neck stood up.

A Shop in Templederry

I was sent to interview the man who started the Here Today chain of small vegetable shops in Dublin. I'm sorry that I can't remember his name. Anyway, they were flying in the city at the time, back in the 1970s, and there was one in Mount Merrion, near the church not far from where he lived. I asked the guy how he got into the business. He said that he was actually an insurance salesman and his patch was in Limerick. But because he was from Howth, he began to take some fresh fish down that way with him and he sold it to a small shop on the way.

'Where was the shop?' I asked.

He said it wasn't important, it was just a small shop in a small village in Tipperary.

'Where?' I asked. I liked details in stories.

'Just outside Nenagh,' he said.

'What was it called?' I asked.

He looked exasperated. 'Templederry,' he said.

I asked the name of the shop though at this stage I think I knew.

'Kennedys,' he said.

'I know it,' I told him. 'My dad was born there and his father ran it...'

He nearly collapsed.

In Templederry Again

Our parasol blew into the next door garden and the man looking after it brought it around a few days later. It was All Ireland Football weekend I think. So he asked me if I was a Dub. I told him I was half Tipp and half Roscommon.

'What part of Tipp?'

As ever, I said it was a small village in the north and that my father had been born there.

He persisted. 'What is it called?'

I told him. Templederry.

'I'm from Templederry. What's your name?'

'Murray,' I said.

'Which Murrays?' he asked.

'Middleplough. My cousins are John and Declan and David and…'

'Is there a Helen?'

'Helena,' I corrected him.

'I was in school with her.'

Amazing. Only I hadn't seen her for years, I said.

Postscript: I popped into my local Hickey's pharmacy the following day. And Helena was there…

At the Stables

It was our first visit to Castle Leslie with Charlotte and she was anxious to do a bit of horse riding. So we went to the stables. We walked along looking at the horses and noting their names. It was unbelievable.

There was Paddy. Next door was Clinton. And finally, Murray. Scary!

Slow Learner

Figuring It Out (1)

When I was about 15 or so, I used to spend a little time with friends in Brittas Bay. On one of those occasions, we all fancied a girl called Susie. I remember well that Amen Corner had a hit at the time called 'Hello Susie'.

Anyway, I asked her out and, to my surprise, she said yes. We were to meet outside the Ambassador Cinema at 7.00 pm one night the following week. I spruced myself up and got there at quarter to. No sign of Susie. 7.00. No sign of Susie. 7.15. No sign of Susie. I began to worry. So I called her. Her dad answered.

'Hello,' I said, 'my name is Patrick and I'm bringing Susie to the pictures tonight. I'm wondering if she has left the house or if she's delayed?'

'The pictures, is it?' her father said. 'She'll be there in a little while.'

And indeed she was. Her father actually dropped her at the door just in time to catch the movie. We never met again ...

... I'd say it was thirty years later when it finally dawned on me. Yes, I know it's obvious now. Susie was standing me up. And when I called, I reckon her dad read her the riot act, told her to get ready and dragged the unfortunate and very reluctant teenager into town to meet me. All those years on, I still had a reddener when I figured it out.

Figuring It Out (2)

By fifth year in Blackrock College, I must have been an utter nightmare. I was a messer. I disrupted classes. I was always in trouble.

Séamus Grace was our English teacher in fifth year. Mr Grace was gentle kind of man. We knew he had spent some years working with the Legion of Mary abroad. A devout man. But he loved English – and chess. And he passed on his love for those subjects to his students. Indeed, he often ignored the curriculum in the opening months of the school year to teach what he thought should be taught. And he wasn't wrong. It is why so many students loved him.

One day, in fifth year, he gave us an essay to be written over the weekend. The title was 'The Agony of Waiting'. I took to the task with gusto, writing an essay about how the Manchester United players behaved as they waited to take to the pitch for the 1968 European Cup Final at Wembley, which had been played the previous May. I was liberal with my use of language. I didn't quite stretch to the 'f' word, but I didn't stop far short. There were a few 'bloodys', one or two 'damns' and possibly even a 'feck'. Essentially, I didn't give a damn. I knew I'd be in trouble. I knew I'd be suspended – again. But I didn't care.

When Mr Grace came in to the classroom the day after we had handed up our essays, he threw mine down in front of me and said: 'Read that out loud.'

I was shocked. I thought this would go beyond suspension and that I might actually be expelled. And indeed, there were a few gasps at the colourful language in the essay. And utter silence when I finished.

And then Mr Grace said: '*That*, gentlemen, is how to write an essay.'

I was astonished. I was amazed. (An unintended consequence, by the way, was a smattering of foul language in half the essays written in the class the following weekend.) So astonished was I that, at least in that one class, I changed my behaviour. It started me on the course which saw me get honours in English in the leaving cert.

Séamus Grace was buried the same day as my mother in 2003. But it was sometime after that, believe it or not, that it finally dawned on me. The essay wasn't that good at all. But Séamus Grace saw a little rebel, a teenager who was on the verge of destroying his life and thought that, maybe, a little praise instead of punishment might go a long way.

It did. To this day I think he saved me. But why did it take so long for me to figure that out?

Four Stories about Archibald Albion FC

A Pissed Fullback

Rugby was my game. But I ended up managing a junior soccer team! The team was called Archibald Albion and I came to be manager because, well, I kind of adopted them in my column in the *Star*. Why? Because they were lousy.

So my colleague Senan Molony, who started the team and named it after the Spurs player Steve Archibald, asked me to go and see them play. I did. And if I remember correctly, he was quite smug at half time because they were winning 3-0. It ended up 3-3. Three own goals. I kid you not. So I became their manager.

We were away to Castleknock Celtic. They kind of fancied themselves. Indeed, when we got there, the Castleknock team were all in their matching, spotless tracksuits doing warm up exercises on the side of the pitch. The Archies, on the other hand, were sitting down in their unwashed gear, half of them smoking.

About ten or fifteen minutes into the game, the referee called me over. He told me he thought my left full back (Paul Mannering, or Manners) was concussed and might have to come off. So I called him over.

'Are you okay?' I asked him.

'I'm pissed,' he said. He'd come straight to the game from a night out! He played on. And we won.

Hillsborough 2

Manners again. I got fed up with just the 13 – the eleven picked on the team and two subs – turning up every week. Anyone left out of the 13 never seemed to come and support the lads. So I issued an edict. Come or you won't be picked. The next game was a cup match in Bushy Park. And, fair dues, about 15 or 16 of the lads turned up. The other team had about ten supporters. So it was the busiest sideline I'd ever seen for the Archies. Then Manners came over to me.

'I'm very worried,' he said.

I wasn't sure what he was on about. 'Worried about what?' I asked him.

He pointed to the fifteen or sixteen supporters on the sideline and said: 'This could be another Hillsborough.'

A Case of Mistaken Identity

I've never loved referees. I could write a book about them. One incident, though, stands out. The Archies were playing in St Anne's Park in Raheny and the referee was particularly awful. I told him so. Loudly. More than once. And so he eventually came over to me and ordered me from the park.

'What?' I said, feigning shock. 'I was just passing through, walking my dog (I pointed) when I saw this match. I stopped to watch and thought to myself, this has to be the worst referee I have ever seen. I thought you were a complete eejit, useless, blind, crap. I don't even know who's playing. I just know you're crap. So, you can't order me from the park, I've nothing to do with the game.'

He looked at me, then he walked away. Was he a bad referee? Well, he didn't notice that a) I didn't actually have a dog and b) I was wearing a t-shirt emblazoned with the words Archibald Albion.

Where's Cardiff?

I couldn't go with them when the lads went to Wales to play a few friendly matches. One was in Cardiff. They hired a coach and headed off to play the game. Only they couldn't find Cardiff. I swear to God. They couldn't find Cardiff.

Ten Bits of Very Bad Luck

Missing Out Big Time

When I was in that Irish college, I was chosen to sing at the big Feis Ceoil in Dublin. That would have meant going all the way to Dublin, on a bus, with teachers and the one or two others who had been selected. It was a great chance. All the way home to Dublin! And maybe returning to Ring in glory.

Only, well, you see the mum and dad of another girl in the college were coming down that weekend. They were friends with my mum and dad. And so it was presumed that they'd take me out with their daughter, Saibh, and her friend Gráinne whose parents also knew mine. So I told the teachers I wouldn't be able to go to the Feis.

The bus left early on Saturday and that afternoon Saibh's parents duly arrived. Only they thought I'd gone to the Feis and didn't ask where I was. So I was on my own for the weekend.

I missed my trip out with Saibh and Gráinne. And I missed out on the Feis.

Fore!

My brother Dee was messing around in the garden with a golf club. He was, I'd say, about ten which means I was about six.

193

He was swinging away pretending to hit a golf ball. It was the start of a lifetime's association with golf.

I must have been impressed. Because I tried to get a closer view. I tried to get a *very* close view. Instead, I got the full strength of the golf club on the forehead as Dee tested his backswing. It swelled up first. Like an egg, then it burst. I needed stiches. And I still have the scar.

Coming Back to Earth

The next year, 1961, I had another little mishap. It came from me rushing to see Yuri Gagarin orbiting the earth. Well, not *see* him exactly. But we were told we could see the light reflecting off his capsule. I stood in the back garden and I saw something moving in the sky. I think. Then I ran through the garage to the front to see it again and tripped over a bike which fell on me. The rubber grip on the handlebars was long gone so the roundy bit on the end hit me on the forehead. And that's where the second scar came from.

Ice Skating Fiasco

James Morrissey has been a friend of mine for yonks. And he's friendly with Des McEvaddy, a serial entrepreneur. Des opened Ireland's first ice rink in a disused cinema in Dolphin's Barn. Not exactly Klosters but ice skating nonetheless.

A few of us went to the opening night and drank some beer, put on skates and off we went. Easy peasy. We were invited back for a private skate a few days later. It was in the morning. There was no beer and only four of us skating. It didn't seem quite so easy.

I slowly moved along the ice and then stopped. My left leg began to slip away. My right stayed rooted in the ice, the blade firmly stuck. My right leg began to twist as the left moved further away. Then it snapped. It was a loud snap my friend and colleague Liam Collins said. I didn't hear it. But I felt it. There wasn't much pain. Adrenalin is a wonderful thing. But they had to call an ambulance. I asked them not to put the siren on. So they did.

It turned out I had broken my tibia and my fibula in several places. So bad was it, I needed a plate inserted to knit the bone back together again. My ice skating career was over. And that's the third scar.

Look Before You Leap

The Blackrock College Scout Troop headed off to Lough Key in Roscommon for its annual camp. At the time, it wasn't the Forest Park it is now. There was a burned down, derelict mansion, unkempt grounds and little else. It looked like nobody had visited for years. Except the harbour.

Not much came in and out of the harbour as it happens. In our week or so there, not one craft visited. That made it ideal for swimming. And so muggins here decided that the best way into the water was to jump in. So jump I did.

I found out the hard way that someone had been there before us. Because stuck in the mud on the floor of the harbour was a bottle. Or rather, half a bottle. The neck was stuck in the mud and the rest of the jagged remains of the glass container was pointing upwards. And I hit it spot on. Cuts on the ball of my foot, in between the toes – lots of them. The fourth, fifth and sixth scars. And the realisation that I should have remembered that old adage. Look before you leap.

Losing All Sense of Time

No injuries this time. Just bad timing. I was at a Grand Prix, a guest of Michael Brady of Marlboro cigarettes. Well, I was a smoker at the time.

We had many great weekends in many great places with Michael. On this occasion, we were in, I think, Barcelona. Wined and dined as ever. There was to be a big dinner after the race, but Michael suggested we miss it.

'It will be packed, people from all over, speeches and what not,' he said.

So we decided to go off as a small group of Irish hacks. I had forgotten that at a previous function we had been asked to predict the 1-2-3-4-5 in the race. The prize was a top-of-the-range Tag Heuer watch.

When we got back on the Sunday night from our Irish hacks-only dinner, a girl in a Marlboro top approached me.

'Are you Paddy Murray?'

I said I was.

'You were the only one who got the 1-2-3-4-5 right in the race,' she said.

I suddenly remembered. The competition. The forecast. *The Tag Heuer Watch worth €10,000!* I smiled.

She didn't. 'Pity you weren't at the dinner,' she said. 'The prize had to go to someone who was there. A Japanese gentleman won,' she said.

An Expensive Kick

Good Friday in 1964. A few of us were playing football on Sycamore Road in Mount Merrion. Just messing around. I kicked a ball. It went high. It went over the wall into the Hickeys' garden. And it kept going. It kept going until it hit the downstairs window and broke it. We could hear the glass shattering. I turned to my friends. Friends? Not a sign of them. All gone.

I went into the house. It was quiet. There was no radio or television in the afternoon back then, and there certainly wasn't anything in the way of 'entertainment' on Good Friday. Nor were there shops open. Newsagents, grocery, butchers, chemists were all firmly locked up for the day. Oh. And glaziers. The chances of finding a glazier on Good Friday in 1964 were pretty much zero.

The Hickeys weren't pleased and who can blame them. The thing is, we didn't know them very well. They lived directly across the road but we didn't know them. You see, they were (deep breath) Lapsed Catholics. Oh yes, Lapsed Catholics. That was *worse* than being a Protestant.

Their window still had to be fixed and my father went off on tour to find a glazier. No Googling glaziers back then. Well, miracles do happen. He found one. I think it cost him £12 to get the thing fixed. And £12 was a lot of money in 1964. A day's pay for the well paid.

As for my friends? I never forgot their running away and leaving me to face the music. Obviously!

Short-armed

Big in-house game in 'Rock in 1970. I haven't the faintest idea which team was which. But I do know what happened. I was a prop. Props weren't noted for speed though I wasn't slow. The game was finely balanced when, all of a sudden, I'm there, through, 25 yards to go and only their full back – I'll just call him Joe – to beat. I knew Joe was quick. But I had the advantage. I had the ball and I knew which way I was going to go. I ran towards him and then I ducked to the left. If I tell you that it took me a full 24 hours to remember who I was, you might figure out what happened. Joe short-armed me. Elbow out, and it got me just under the chin. I was out cold.

That evening, I sat at the wrong table in the refectory for our evening meal. I had no idea what overnight work we'd been given. I got people's names wrong. My brain was mush. There are a number of lessons here: 1) Concussion was a problem in rugby even back then, 2) Nice guys, Joe was one, will short arm you if they have to, 3) Props should pass it if they're able to.

And the worst thing about it? I didn't get the try.

Striking Out

Mick Flannery sings the line: I'm no ladies man. Well, I'm not. But twice, what seemed like good luck has turned bad on me in that area of my life.

The first was in Italy. We were on a continental trip with the Blackrock College 44th Scout Troop. We'd been to London, Munich, Innsbruck and now we were on the Italian coast at La Spezia.

We hit the beach and for some reason, myself and one other guy hit it off with two local girls of our own age, about 15. Nellie was one and the other, the girl I linked up with, was Roberta. We had a great afternoon and arranged to meet them again the following day. We had two more days in La Spezia. Or so we thought.

Because for reasons that aren't quite clear, though I have my suspicions, our stay in La Spezia was cut short. 'We're going to Grenoble tonight,' we were all told.

We asked if we could look for the girls to say goodbye. But we were told we couldn't. Bit of an overreaction.

And then, a year or so later, we were on a Venture Scout trip to the west of Ireland. Westport, I think, though it might have been Castlebar. Again, through sheer luck and certainly not due to looks or charm, me and one other guy, Peter – he who had won the place I had hoped for on the Junior Cup Team – linked up with two local girls.

'We'll see you later,' we said and then, when later came and against instructions from our 'leader', who was a year ahead of us in school, we met them.

When we returned, not late, before dark, we were told to pack, that we were going home and our parents had been in-formed. *You what?* The bastard rang our parents to rat on us. So we had to get the train home the next day. At least we were pretty sure of the motivation that time. Jealousy.

Missed Out

I should be resting at my mansion in the south of France, with my Ferrari parked beside the swimming pool.

I worked with John Lloyd back in the 1970s. John Lloyd, as you will recall, was involved with a programme on BBC Radio 4 called *Weekending*. It was a topical satirical show and John was one of the producers. When he moved on to make the *New Huddlines* with comedian Roy Hudd, I moved with him and wrote scripts for that radio show. Indeed, I attended some of the recordings. I should have stuck with John. He went on to make *Not the Nine O'Clock news*, *Spitting Image* and many other shows.

Back here, I worked on the *Twink Show*. It was actually pretty good and very funny. And who was running the show? John McColgan and Moya Doherty. Dammit, I should have stuck with them too. If only I'd stuck to the Irish dancing when I was in Irish college.

Ten Stories about Music

VIP

Being press, we often wore VIP badges at the Slane gigs when we were up around the castle. At the Queen gig, I decided I'd have a peek at how ordinary concert goers were getting on. I was sorry I did.

I walked through the crowd and in various places saw: Couples openly having sex. People apparently in comas from drink or drugs. People vomiting all over the place. One bloke having a piss right in the middle of the crowd. And a couple of blokes beating the shite out of each other. I didn't like it. I liked it even less when I heard a voice muttering, 'VIP me bollocks.' I made a hasty retreat back to the castle.

Sweet Payback

I was bringing some friends back to Dublin after the gig one year when the clutch in my old banger started acting up. It was going to be a long trip home. I pulled into a petrol station in the hope that a mechanic would be on duty. Not a chance.

Then a car pulled up at the pump alongside. It was, well, someone reasonably well known and known to me. So I asked him if he'd mind giving a few of my friends a lift – I had noticed his car was carrying just him and one passenger.

'Sorry, I'm not going that way,' he said before I told him where they were going. He drove off.

About six weeks later, I got a call in the newsroom. It was the same guy. He told me that he was up in court that day on a minor drugs charge and asked if I could make sure it didn't get into the paper. I didn't know he was due in court on a minor drugs charge and neither did anyone else until he told us. It was just a little story. Down the side of page one.

'Do Wah Diddy'

It was 2002 and I was doing a piece for the *Tribune* on the 40th anniversary of RTÉ first broadcasting an Irish Top Ten. Larry Gogan and I, along with Brendan Balfe, chatted about various things that happened over the years, including the number of songs which were banned. These included Manfred Mann's 'Do Wah Diddy'.

'Why was that banned?' I asked Larry.

'Too much Diddy and not enough Do Wah,' said Larry.

The Almost

I was in a band once. We were called The Almost. John Philip Murray was on drums. Dave Fleming on lead guitar. Neil McHugh on bass. Ciaran Stacey on rhythm. Me on rhythm and vocals. We were all from Mount Merrion and we rehearsed mostly in our house.

The Barn was where we played. It was the Mount Merrion parish 'hop'. A 'hop' is what eventually came to be called a disco, or a rave, or whatever it is now. (We also played at an orphanage in Kill O'the Grange. And I think the biggest crowd we ever had was in a school in Cabra. It was the school for the deaf. Yeh. I know.)

We played The Barn several times. I know we sang songs likes 'Willow Tree', 'Rag Doll', 'We Shall Not Be Moved', 'For Your Love' ...

Anyway, Ciaran and I were eventually replaced by Kevin Moore and his brother Tommy. We could have been Pete Best and Stuart Sutcliffe only The Almost never became the Beatles.

I remember one night we played The Barn, and the girls screamed and we were cheered and applauded and, well, the head swelled. I was 12. I asked this girl to dance. She was 14. I fancied her. And I can still see her face. Anyway, I was full of myself. So I danced away and eventually asked her, 'What age do you think I am?'

'Twelve,' she said.

Lord, how small I felt.

Eventually Ciaran and I were fired and replaced by the Moore brothers. Why were we fired? Musical differences. The main difference being that the other lads could play their instruments and we couldn't.

Horslips at Blackrock Park

It was August 1971. The sixties had arrived a little late in Ireland. When most of the western world was taking Timothy Leary's advice and tuning in, turning on and dropping out as they listened to Jimi Hendrix, the Grateful Dead and the Doors, most Irish, eh, music lovers were still packing the ballrooms to hear the Clipper Carlton, the Capital Showband and the Gay Stars who probably wouldn't call themselves that now. But back to Blackrock Park on August the 8th, 1971.

We'd had a little taste of an outdoor music event the previous year when Mungo Jerry played Richmond Park in Inchicore. But this, well, it had more of a festival feel about it and it allowed us to pretend. The concert – it was long before they were called gigs – was called Rock in the Hollow and it was headlined by Phil Lynott and Thin Lizzy. Also on the bill that day were Horslips, Elmer Fudd, Gypsy Rock, Mellow Candle and the inevitable Supply, Demand and Curve.

We were about 383,000 short of the attendance at Woodstock two years earlier. There was no mud. And everybody kept their clothes on. But something momentous did happen that day. Horslips kind of stole the show and the following spring decided to turn professional. Not long afterwards, they received a call from McConnell's advertising agency which had sent a photographer to our little Woodstock in Blackrock Park.

They asked Horslips to take part in an ad campaign aimed at what they called the youth market. They wanted the band to headline a similar free concert which would be filmed for an advertisement which would only ever be seen in cinemas. That, at least, was the promise. The money on offer meant they could buy their own PA equipment. And *that* made it all worthwhile and they weren't really selling their souls.

The band members took some persuading. But hadn't the Beatles endorsed Lybro jeans and the Rolling Stones and the Who endorsed Coke – the kind you drink from a bottle. The really bad bit though was that Horslips would have to mime to a dodgy jingle written and performed by some session musicians in Germany.

So they did the festival on the back lot at Ardmore studios where among the support acts was a chap called Chris Davison in a stars and stripes suit. The crowd was given crisps, ice-cream and soft drinks. Definitely not Woodstock.

Some time later, the ad went out. Only in cinemas? Well, yes, until *Reelin' in the Years* discovered it and now everyone has seen Horslips singing about Mirinda. Soon after, guitarist Declan Sinnott left the band to be replaced by Johnny Fean. And onwards and upwards they went – and they're flying high once more. And it all began that afternoon in August 1971 at our little Woodstock in the Hollow in Blackrock Park.

Fleetwood Mac at the National Stadium

Despite my being a disobedient brat, my mother and father tried to and did keep a fairly close eye on me. So I have no idea how I managed to get to the National Stadium on a weeknight in October 1969 to see Peter Green's Fleetwood Mac. But I did and it was one of the greats. Peter and Jeremy Spencer weren't in the band for much longer, but that night it was like a guitar duel between them. The band played for just short of four hours.

Apart from the music, one of the things the gig is famous for is the fact that, at the end, the cleaning ladies were dancing around their brushes waiting for the band to finish.

We must have walked home too – the buses ended much earlier back then. What lie I told when I got home, I can't recollect. But either it was brilliant or, more likely, my mother and father knew it was a lie and decided to say nothing...

Calling Radio Luxembourg

London, 1972, I think. Brendan (Beamish) Martin and I had a few drinks and were walking around West London before I went back to the house my brother was renting in Kingsbury and Brendan returned to where he was living – in a tent belonging to Christian Aid or some such, at Wormwood Scrubs.

We walked along Hertford Street and noticed that one of the buildings was the HQ and studios of Radio Luxembourg. Beamish quite rightly pointed out that they'd been filling our heads with music for years. It was our turn. So, he said, let's sing in the letter box. And so we did. We leaned down and started singing in the letter box. They we heard a voice behind us. A strong Cockney voice. It belonged to a bobby.

'Wot you doing then?' he asked.

'Eh, we're putting in a request,' Beamish replied.

'A request?' said the bobby. 'Who's the request for?'

'My girlfriend,' said Beamish.

'Your girlfriend?' repeated the bobby. 'Where do you live?'

'Em. Wormwood Scrubs,' said Beamish.

'*Wormwood Scrubs*!' said the now incredulous bobby. 'Where in Wormwood Scrubs?'

'In a tent,' said Beamish.

The bobby scratched his head, looked around, and walked away. I reckon he had figured that if he brought us to the station and said he had found a guy who lived in a tent at Wormwood Scrubs singing in the letter box of Radio Luxembourg, he might have been arrested himself.

Some Great Gigs

I actually did see XTC in McGonagles and John Sebastian in the Baggot Inn. And my wife Connie saw REM in the SFX and The Ramones in the Television Club. They also played in the State Cinema in Phibsboro. But Dublin had many more mad gigs in the early years. Of course the Beatles and the Stones both played the Adelphi Cinema. Johnny Cash did a gig in the Crystal Ballroom. AC/DC played in the Olympic Ballroom. Bob Marley played Dalymount. Mungo Jerry played Richmond Park. Metallica played in SFX. Public Enemy played McGonagles as did Ozzy Osbourne. And The Boomtown Rats played Dun Laoghaire Town Hall.

Interviewing Your Hero

Despite the biographies after his death pointing out that John Lennon could be a terrible bollocks (I think there was a clue in the song 'Getting Better': 'I used to be cruel to my woman I beat her and kept her apart from the things that she loved') musically, he was a hero. So on my first visit to New York in 1980, I tried to set up an interview. I didn't think it was totally hopeless. He had ties to Ireland and *Double Fantasy*, his comeback album, was just out. I went through his lawyers and they gave me further hope. The problem was, I was tight for time on an *Indo* funded trip, I couldn't hang around. So despite positive noises, I had to leave New York without the interview. Lucky me.

The more I read of his interviews, the more I realized it wouldn't have ended well. Because I am primarily a Beatles fan and since I would have asked him about The Beatles, I think the interview would have ended with him telling me to fuck off. And me telling people never to meet their heroes.

The Failed Busker

I was in another band too – for a week. It was at the Festival of Kerry in Tralee in, I think, 1971. Three of us, me, the girlfriend of a friend and another guy I never saw again, played in O'Connor's of the Square. I don't think it's still there. We sang there every night and packed the place largely, I think, because we more or less abandoned traditional music for The Beatles! The only pay we got was pints!

So we played out on the street a few times to see if we could raise some money. Problem was, there were more freelance collectors going around than there were friends of ours collecting for us. I wouldn't mind, but at three or four in the morning, I had to walk the five miles to Fenit to where I was staying. Don't think I was made for showbiz!

Nine Stories Featuring Food

Losing My Appetite

Back then, in 1973 when I had just started in the *Indo*, I didn't know where to go to eat on my evening break. I was trying to get used to the place and people and wasn't confident enough to ask anyone to join me or which was the best place locally to get a bite to eat. So, occasionally, I went to a certain restaurant near the *Indo* offices on O'Connell Street which was at least tolerable.

One night I sat at the counter. I ordered my food – a fry or fish and chips or some such – paid, and waited for it to be served. A dog strayed in from O'Connell Street, raised a leg and pissed against the corner of the counter.

A uniformed lady in her sixties emerged from behind the counter wearing rubber gloves and carrying a cloth. She wiped up the puddle of piss with the cloth and then, as she walked back to the sink, nonchalantly wiped the counter with the cloth leaving a long, pissy streak on it.

I left. I suddenly wasn't hungry. And I never went back.

Another Lost Customer

There was a café opposite the *Indo*. It was called The Ritz. Occasionally I got a takeaway there. Then, one night, I saw a couple of the more senior reporters looking out the window and occasionally pointing and laughing. I joined them. I had grown a little bit more confident and asked what was going on. There was a kind of ledge above the large sign bearing the café's name.

'There's another...' one of them suddenly said, pointing.

And then I saw it too. A rat. A minute later, another. In ten minutes looking out the window, I saw six rats running along the ledge. And, just like its neighbour above, I never went back.

Daly's Steak House

Now there was some great grub around – even back then. So when I could afford it, I'd go to Daly's Steak House on Eden Quay. Top class fare.

One evening I was sitting at the bar, just beside the serving hatch when the waitress brought back a plate with a steak and all the trimmings still on it. She knocked on the hatch. It opened. She put the plate just inside and said: 'Could you change that sirloin to a fillet?'

Two hands appeared and made a gesture over the plate. A voice boomed: 'Abraca-fuckin-dabra.' And the doors slammed shut.

A Drinkin' House

The Bachelor on Bachelor's Walk was one of our haunts. It served an excellent pint. Occasionally, one of us – usually Tommy – would have cheese and crackers while he supped his pint. Lunch, don't you know. Seán was a barman in the Batch, as we called it. He didn't like the idea of food in pubs. He didn't like the sign over the bar advertising ham and or cheese sandwiches. He just about tolerated the cheese and crackers.

So he wasn't happy when, one day, a small group of middle-aged Americans arrived in and loudly asked for a whole range of sandwiches from ham to cheese and back.

Seán said. 'This is a drinkin' house. But if you go out that door and take a left, you're at O'Connell Street and you can go up and down both sides of it and you'll find eatin' houses everywhere. But like I said, this is a drinkin' house. Fuck off.'

They did. But I often wonder what they told their friends in the States when they got home.

Michelin Contender

And on that subject. The Headline at Leonard's Corner is, I am told, still a fine pub. But years ago it was very ordinary as was the clientele. It was pints, G&Ts (your choice was Cork or Gordon's) or whiskey. And you could get a sandwich.

One day I walked in and saw menus on each table. Proper, colourful, printed menus in plastic containers which stood on the tables. I was curious. I picked one up. Sure enough, it said 'Menu' at the top. And then it said:

'Wide choice of sandwiches. Ham, Cheese or tomato. Ham and cheese, ham and tomato. Cheese and tomato, cheese and ham. Ham, cheese and tomato. All available toasted.'

How they never got a Michelin star....

The Friendly House

It was July 1979 when the Chinese Triad wars came to Dublin. On the night of the 17th, two Chinese men were stabbed to death. One was found bleeding outside a restaurant on Middle Abbey Street called The New Universal, the other was left to die outside the Rotunda Hospital by men who didn't know it was a maternity hospital. The Abbey Street victim was photographed by the *Irish Independent* photographer, the late Art O'Callaghan, who had just left Higgins' pub, another regular haunt for *Indo* staff.

It was a once off though no one doubts that the triads didn't go away, they just learned to keep their head down. But I remember working on the story the next day. I was asked to find out how many Chinese people lived in Ireland. On the basis that every town and village seemed to have at least one Chinese restaurant, I thought the figure would be in the hundreds.

I called the embassy. And the answer I was given was: 'Seven.' We assumed all the others were British.

Dublin humour had a field day with suggestions that some Chinese restaurants were now advertising 'shepherd's pie – made with real shepherds'. And others had finger bowls for any spare fingers which might be found around and about.

But all those wags were outdone by the Chinese themselves. Knowing the name The New Universal was now associated with a brutal murder, the Abbey Street restaurant, when it eventually reopened, was renamed The Friendly House.

Stung Again

Dobbins restaurant, off Mount Street in Dublin 2, was legendary, as was its owner John O'Byrne. John was as decent as they come – somewhat like Patrick Guilbaud (though he didn't cook!) with a touch of Brendan Grace, a slice of Bill Cullen and a sprinkling of Arthur Daley. A terrific host. You couldn't have made Johnny up.

For example: I was standing at a bus stop in Sandymount when I saw a large, vintage Jaguar approach. It pulled in and the passenger door opened. It was Johnny offering me a lift. So we headed into town chatting as we did.

'Lovely car,' I said.

'Would you like to buy it?' Johnny asked. Seriously.

On one occasion in Dobbins, a few of us were having lunch and Johnny came over and sat with us for a chat and as he left recommended a bottle of something or other.

'I'll get it for you,' he said.

And he did. And it *was* special. When the bill arrived, there was something like £100 on it for the wine. Now, bearing in mind we were paying about £30 for really good wine that was a lot. And anyway, Johnny had got it for us, hadn't he? We called the waiter.

'Em, Mr O'Byrne bought that wine for us,' we said.

'I don't know anything about that,' the waiter said.

'Well, can you ask him?' we said.

'I'm afraid he left about an hour ago,' the waiter said.

We'd been stung. Again. The food was terrific, the atmosphere was fantastic and Johnny was great company. Like so many of the good things from then, it is no more.

One-legged Turkey

Dermot Higgins was the proprietor of the pub which bore his name on Abbey Street. We were regulars. To keep it that way, one year Dermot had a series of raffles with the prize in each being a turkey. I was there a lot. I bought a lot of tickets and I won four turkeys.

I kept two for family and gave the others away, one to my colleague James Morrissey. He was chuffed and, after collecting it from the place in the pub where we picked up our prizes, brought it home to Mayo and proudly handed it over. The wrapping was taken off. There was a leg missing. He had brought home a one-legged turkey. I think another colleague may be guilty of the theft of the other leg. I have my suspicions.

Welsh Wanker

It was the Festival in Tralee in the late 1970s or early 1980s. And for some reason, a gang of us linked up with a bunch of Welsh guys. One day, we decided we'd all go for a drink or two and a bite to eat in Lynch's at Spa, a couple of miles from Tralee. So we had a few pints, maybe three or four, and sat to eat. Some had a starter, most had a beautiful steak, some had dessert. Most had a drop of wine. The bill arrived.

One of the Welsh guys had a look and said: 'It's £330, so that's £23 each, make it £25 a head and that will cover for a tip.' Or something along those lines.

We all began looking for our share, chatting as we did. And then a Welsh voice spoke.

'I didn't have the dessert.'

Silence fell. You could see the shock on the faces of the other Welsh guys.

'Well, I didn't. But it's okay. I'll pay the £25.'

'It's okay,' said the guy who had calculated our bill.

'Look, I don't mind,' said the Didn't-Have-Dessert guy.

'No,' said the first Welsh guy. *'You don't have to pay anything.'*

Without being told to, we all added another couple of pounds to our contribution. We returned to Tralee and by eight o'clock that evening none of the Welsh guys were talking to 'Didn't-Have-Dessert' guy. And rightly so.

Four Stories about Mirabeau Restaurant

Sean Kinsella's Mirabeau Restaurant stood on the seafront in Sandycove for a little more than ten years. The stories from it are the stuff of legend. It hosted the likes of Neil Diamond, Demis Roussos, Michael Caine, Laurence Olivier, Burt Lancaster, Richard Burton and many others. It also hosted me, on a few occasions. These are the ones I remember.

Ditching the Unwelcome

Sean hosted what was described as 'a reception' for Peter Kavanagh, brother of Patrick and protector of the poet's legacy. Everything was normal for a little while. And then I heard a kind of 'Psst' noise. I looked around. Nothing.

Then I heard it again. 'Pssst.'

It came from behind a curtain. I was beckoned. Behind the curtain were colleagues like Michael Hand, James Morrissey, Liam Collins and a few others. We were in hiding from the 'riff raff' – other colleagues who weren't among the privileged being invited to stay on for proper food. And of course, drink. So when the last of the unwelcomed left – they had no idea we

were still there – out we came and drank our heads off for the
rest of the night.

Getting Us Home

On another late occasion, when the drinking and eating had
all stopped, we were walked to the door by Sean. It was the
early hours. Most had called taxis to get them home. As each
taxi arrived Sean would hold the door open for the guest who
was leaving after the long night.

One or two were driving – it was the early eighties and
such a thing was still 'acceptable' in some company – and Sean
held the car doors open for them to get in.

But Liam Collins explained to Sean that he had come by
bike. It was chained to the railings outside the restaurant.
Liam took the bike down. Sean took it from him and he held it
while Liam climbed on!

Not the Duck

Then there was the night a few hacks and some partners were
invited for a bite to eat. Sean liked duck. He liked cooking
duck. He liked serving duck. And as we weren't paying, when
he came to each of us and asked us if duck was okay for the
main course, we said yes. Except for one. The wife of one colleague, I won't name her, was asked if she would like some
duck.

'Fuck the duck,' she said. 'I want fillet steak.'

She was, for some time after that, known as 'Fuck the
Duck'.

Rolls Royce in Ballymun

Finally there was the competition. Sean suggested to the then
Herald editor Niall Hanley a competition for his readers.

'Dinner for two in the Mirabeau,' he said.

And if that wasn't enough – it's a prize most Dubliners would have killed for – Sean added: 'And I'll collect the winners in the Rolls Royce.'

So the entries piled in. And one day, Niall asked me to get them so we could pick a winner. Now this wasn't something with which Niall would normally concern himself. Getting the competition right, yes. Marketing it, yes. Presenting it well in the paper, of course. But picking the winner? Anyway, I got the big sack of entries and brought them to Niall's office. He said he'd give me a shout. Twenty minutes or so later, he did. I went in to his office. He was laughing.

'I have the winner,' he said.

And he showed me the entry. The winner was from one of the tower blocks in Ballymun.

'Can't wait to see Sean drive out there in the Roller!'

PART 4 – NEARING THE END . . .

Health and Miracles

If you had asked me how I would react to a bad diagnosis, before I actually got it, I would have told you 'with tears, panic and an overwhelming feeling of self-pity'. But when I was given the news, in November 1998, I surprised myself. Because I was calm, almost relieved – and very optimistic. I had only gone to see this dermatologist at the urging of a friend, because what I believed to be my chronic psoriasis was getting worse. Had my friend, Michael, not urged me, prodded me, annoyed me into going to the doctor that day, I may very well have continued to think that all I had was psoriasis. And I would certainly not have lived for much longer. But I went.

I had been playing a little bit of Taverners' Cricket at Terenure Sports Club or CYM as most people still seem to know it. But I told Michael I was giving it up. The communal shower after the games had become embarrassing. I was covered in blotches and people couldn't help staring at the blotches and I couldn't help looking at them staring at me and everyone ended up embarrassed.

So Michael pushed me into going to the dermatologist. I made an appointment with Dr Rosemary Watson in Blackrock Clinic. It was on the second visit that I got the news. I had something called Cutaneous T-Cell Lymphoma (CTCL). Lymphoma. I knew that word.

'Cancer,' the doctor said, just in case I was in any way confused. 'Our aim,' she added that day, 'is to treat you so that, with a bit of luck, you will die with this disease, not of it.

She let the news sink in and then asked me how I felt. And from nowhere came this bit of profundity!

'There will be a man on a bus passing this clinic today and he'll be dead within a week. He doesn't know there's anything wrong with him. I'm lucky, because I know what's wrong and I know it's going to be treated.'

And that's what happened. There is no point pretending that it's an easy journey. There are times when it has been absolutely bloody awful. And I have seen many people, friends and relatives, die from cancers of various kinds over these past 22 years and wondered why I am lucky enough to be alive.

Certainly, the extraordinary treatment I have received in our oft maligned health service has played its part. You might doubt it, but the odd prayer may have helped too. Mock if you like, but it works for me.

Medically, it was a series of treatments, luck, minor miracles and major interventions. Photophersis was first. That's where your blood is taken out, irradiated, and put back in. All that happened in Belfast's City Hospital because at the time it wasn't done in the south so required a fortnightly trip north.

For a while, it worked, but like many treatments its effectiveness eventually diminished. And so next came Full Body Electron Beam treatment. This too, was done in Belfast and while it was easy enough at the start, the last few treatments hurt like hell. Chemotherapy followed and that held things at bay for a while. There followed a trip to London to see a specialist who, if I remember correctly, didn't offer any solutions.

Then there was chemo until the disease affected my hands and feet so badly that Christmas 2007 was a misery. Christmas Day was spent lying on a couch, with a brief interlude for a half-eaten dinner. My hands and feet were covered in sores, bandaged and almost impossible to use. Walking was painful and typing or writing were all but impossible.

Treatment followed treatment. A drug called Targretin was introduced and it seemed to do the trick – for a while. Then it was Zolinza – these names are burned into my memory – a trial drug which didn't work at all, at least for me. A tumour developed on my foot and treatment after treatment failed not just to get rid of it, but to stop it growing. It actually festered to the point where one doctor, admittedly a junior, suggested that the foot might have to be amputated.

It took a mixture of drugs to see it off. It was pot luck, in a way. They threw everything at it. And something worked.

Another trip to London followed and on this occasion and for the first time a Bone Marrow Transplant was mentioned. Indeed, it was suggested that I might actually have the transplant in London – and soon. The whole notion was frightening. I knew I was sick. But sick enough for such a treatment?

My haematologist, Dr Elisabeth Vandenberghe, suggested I have the transplant in St James' Hospital in Dublin. My siblings all volunteered as donors, but sadly none provided a match. At one point, when Dr Vandenberghe was off, I saw another doctor. She asked me if I was worried. I told her I was. About what, she asked. I said I was worried about the prospect of a transplant. She asked why. I told her I was afraid that if I had a transplant, I might die.

She replied quickly: 'You'll die if you don't have one.'

I like that kind of frankness.

But in early 2008, I was told that I was to have the transplant in May and I did. The donor was, I believe, German. I am not permitted to know his or her identity. It seems like an age ago.

I can't pretend that my life now is the same as that of a healthy man of my age. My lymphoma is at bay but apparently it's still there somewhere, lurking. I have a small difficulty with my eyes, a tiny problem of dryness caused by Graft Versus Host Disease – when foreign matter is introduced to your body it may continue to fight it, even at a low level. I had diabetes, caused entirely by drugs. Now it's gone. More good luck.

But I have COPD Stage 4 – and there's no Stage 5. They tell me that a Bone Marrow Transplant can trigger latent respiratory problems. Well, so can smoking. And that's what I'm blaming for my COPD. Decades of paying out good money to damage my health. I haven't smoked for 12 years or so, but there were too many cigarettes over my lifetime.

So I can't play football in the park with Charlotte, can't climb a mountain with her, can't go on long walks. I can't fly to New York with Connie and Charlotte and walk down Fifth Avenue with them and go into Tiffany's and buy something – small – for Charlotte. That was an ambition. That was *the* item on my bucket list.

Not being able to do that one thing with my wife and daughter breaks my heart. But I have adjusted my life. It's what you do when you have illness. You adapt. You change the way you live. You make allowances for yourself. You try not to do things you can't do, so as not to disappoint yourself. You appreciate what you have and stop complaining about what you don't have.

But mostly, what you do is appreciate everything. Books. Films. Nature. People. You find yourself noticing good things, good people, good news. You find yourself rediscovering music and language, the Irish language in particular, and the beautiful country I live in (I have to appreciate it, I'm advised against flying so I can't go anywhere else!).

I am extraordinarily lucky. Connie and I are lucky to be alive and to have a beautiful daughter so many years after both of us were diagnosed with life-threatening illnesses. Living with cancer? It might not be easy, but, personally, I think it's absolutely bloody wonderful. And what makes it all the more wonderful for me is, essentially, parts two and three of this particular tale.

You see, six months or so after I was diagnosed, Connie – my then partner who became my wife – suffered a brain haemorrhage. It was Easter Weekend and Connie had spent the day with colleagues from *The Star* working for free for a newspaper associated with RTÉ's Telethon.

They had gone for a few drinks afterwards and I was at home in bed. I heard her taxi pulling up and saw Connie crossing the road. She staggered. I'd never seen her do that before. I let her in and she went straight to the bedroom. And as she stood by the bed, Connie suddenly said:

'Something is happening to me.'

I noticed her movements had become jerky. I rang my doctor's emergency number but because Connie wasn't a patient, there was no help available! So I called 999.

The ambulance arrived and Connie, now almost comatose, was brought down to it in a chair and we headed for St James's hospital. Connie was put on a trolley. Hours later a doctor saw her. Clearly, there was still a whiff of alcohol and he said that was her problem. Alcohol. I protested. But he told me to take her home. Hours and hours wasted.

By the following morning Connie was no better. So I managed to get her to the car and drove back to James's. I brought her to A&E and sat her down. I was told there was a queue. I was now pretty sure that she was seriously ill. So, quite loudly, I mentioned that we had been there the previous day and she had been sent home and she was extremely ill and… It worked. Back into the emergency ward on a trolley.

This time, a young doctor came to see Connie. It took him about a minute to decide to send her for a scan. And it took not very much more time for him to come back and tell us she had had a bleed on her brain. It was decided to send her to Beaumont Hospital where they specialised in head injuries and the like. I wasn't allowed go in the ambulance (which actually broke down on the way). I stood outside A&E crying and crying. I called a few people to tell them through my tears what had happened.

In Beaumont, it was suggested that there wasn't much hope. I remember one consultant asking a barely conscious Connie who the prime minister was. 'Tony Blair,' she replied. Well, she said much later, if he'd asked who the Taoiseach was I would have said Bertie. But she knew the day of the week and so on. Nonetheless, I was told to say near my phone. The first problem was getting her through the night.

Every day was fraught for a while. Every day brought the risk of Connie dying. And when she eventually moved from Intensive Care to High Dependency, we got the news that she would require brain surgery.

Friends called to see her. She was particularly chuffed when Eddie Irvine dropped in. He made the effort to come to the hospital and sit with her. It lifted her spirits.

The operation was a success but the pain she was in after it was extreme. She sat in the bed holding her head just waiting until the morphine pump, which was on a timer, allowed her to give herself another shot. She was in hospital for seven long weeks and she left in a wheelchair.

The recovery took a long, long time and left Connie with some slight but permanent disabilities. But her courage saw her through. And when she was better, we addressed the next item on the agenda. Starting a family.

Before I had started treatment in Belfast which, I had been told, would leave me infertile, I had left a sperm sample at the HARI institute in the Rotunda Hospital. I hadn't told Connie. But I did now. And so we set out on the IVF route which, after a couple of failures, delivered Charlotte.

Connie's waters broke on St Patrick's Day and I remember it taking us hours to get to the Rotunda with the parade blocking off the city and Parnell Square in particular. It was weeks later that Charlotte arrived, early, small but so extraordinarily beautiful.

So doctors saved me. Doctors saved Connie. Doctors helped us make Charlotte. And scoff if you like, and many will, but our local church now is the Passionist Monastery at Mount Argus. And I discovered that buried there are the remains of Charles of Mount Argus, then Blessed, now Saint. I have turned to him more than once through various illnesses and trials and throughout Connie's pregnancy. Charlotte is named after him – well, partly. Connie admits she agreed to the name because of the Cure song, 'Charlotte Sometimes'!

And I don't know about the other two, but I'm so glad that with the help of doctors – and St Charles – I have lived much of my life with the two most beautiful people who ever graced this planet, two people I have loved more than life itself. And didn't it just take a miracle for us all to be here.

A Kind of Abandonment

There is no adage truer than 'out of sight, out of mind'. If you're ill, long term, you learn that very quickly. I remember many years ago, a friend of mine was involved in a fatal traffic accident. He was the driver. Two of our mutual friends died. It was, of course, big news in the newspapers.

The next day, I was told Kevin, the driver, had asked for me so I went to visit. There was a scrum. 'Friends' from everywhere crammed around the bed. But only days later, just days, there I was alone with him. Many of those 'friends' never appeared again, their curiosity sated. Long-term illness has a strange and similar effect. Some friends you expect to see on a regular basis, you don't see much of at all.

Family, you certainly see. At least I certainly saw my family. Best in the world. Contact every day and visits when I wanted them.

Friends? Well, though they were kind, though they did everything I wanted, I managed to pass year after year hardly seeing anyone from work. Rarely even a telephone call. You forget sometimes that people have their own lives to get on with. Or maybe it's because when push comes to shove I'm a bit of an eejit.

Does that mean they didn't care? No, I don't think that's fair. They had their own lives. Some tell you they don't 'do hospitals' and they probably don't. Others promised but, well, just never got around to it. And for many others, it was 'out of sight, out of mind' which might have been just as well.

The look on some of the faces of those who hadn't seen me for ages was something as I was now 30 kilos lighter. No doubt they were subconsciously making funeral arrangements while telling me how well I looked. I suppose part of me enjoyed their disomfort.

Winding Down

I suppose you could say I'm winding down. It's early 2020. Three of my twelve doctors have admitted to me that they thought I would be long dead by now. They cannot explain how I am alive with all the illnesses from which I suffer. Just before Christmas 2019, I put my respiratory consultant on the spot.

'Will I be here this time next year?'

He said he didn't know.

'Your best guess?'

'No. You won't.'

Another pessimistic prognosis. I always say three things keep me alive. Positivity, music and whingeing!

I try to get to a couple of gigs a month but missed five in recent months due to illness and missed even more because of Covid-19. My breathing is deteriorating rapidly. Everything is difficult. But I'm alive. And the plan is to stay that way as long as possible.

Helping me, is my team!

- Haematologist (Blood specialist for my lymphoma)

- Pulmonologist (Respiratory specialist for my COPD)

- Dermatologist (Skin specialist because my lymphoma manifested itself on my skin)

- Ophthalmologist (Slight after-affect on my eyes after my Bone Marrow Transplant)

- Otolaryngologist (Throat specialist to deal with narrowing of the throat)

- Gastroenterologist (Few polyps around my innards!)

- Orthopaedic specialist (neck) (Bone specialist for disintegrating bone in the neck due to necrosis)

- Orthopaedic specialist (shoulder) (Bone specialist disintegrating bone in the shoulder due to necrosis)

- Endocrinologist (To check for diabetes which I had due to drugs following Bone Marrow Transplant but which is currently at bay.)

- Cardiologist (Heart specialist for Atrial Fibrillation)

- GP for everything and to keep it all together.

Enough for a soccer team *and* a sub!

The Cruellest Part

Death is, of course, cruel. But there are three aspects of death that are more cruel than others. The first is that, though I am Christian and believe there is another life after life on earth, I don't really see it that you switch off one and switch on the other kind of instantly. In other words, you don't die and get to sit on the branch of a high tree watching those you love forever more.

The second is that memory dies with you. You can't even keep the wonderful, beautiful memories, which you have spent a lifetime storing in your brain. That I cannot go to my grave with a picture of my daughter etched on my brain for eternity is more heartbreaking than anything else.

Which brings me to the third thing. Missing those you love is hard. But in death, you don't even get to do that. You don't even get to have the pain of missing them. And that's the worst thing of all.

God

There will always be people who don't just doubt the existence of God, but actively campaign to change the beliefs of those who have no such doubts or who, like most of us, have occasional doubts. But for me, God is an important part of my life.

I don't think I ever actually stopped believing in God at any time. Certainly, through my teens and twenties and maybe even my thirties I ignored Him. (You can see by the capital letter on Him, that I am firm believer now.) I ignored God and religion because it didn't suit me. Much the same reason many people do today. Who wants rules that stop you doing things? And I can't even remember how, when or why it call came back to me. But it did.

I see the proof of His existence everywhere. Others look at exactly the same things and point them as proof there is no God.

I have seen Richard Dawkins, talking out of both sides of his mouth, wondering what kind of God it was that permitted pain and suffering. What kind of God, Richard? But there is no God! At least, you say there isn't.

Dawkins strikes me as the kind whose problem is not that he doesn't believe in God, but that God, he thinks, doesn't believe in him. He strikes me as the kind who wants proof positive. He strikes me as the kind who will not believe until he has had a personal audience.

One of the finest pieces I ever read appeared in Dublin's *Sunday Independent*, written by Jonathan Philbin Bowman, not long before his tragic death. This is it.

> The whole thing about God is, I don't know why people need miracles to prove anything. It seems to me that fingernails are a miracle. The fact that if you're lucky and your child is okay, they get born with five on each hand. Fingernails! I mean, who came up with fingernails? And put them just there at the end? And let them grow, and made them hard and different chemically from flesh? That's enough of a miracles.

I could try and try and try. But I could never put it any better than Jonathan did.

Being Sure

We went to Mass in Mount Argus, in Dublin. On one particular Sunday, a priest who I think was from Belfast, told the story about his mother and her last hours. He called to see her and she was visibly upset. He asked her what was wrong. She was, she told him, worried about what would happen to her after she died. He reassured her.

'You went to Mass every day of your life Mother. You were devout. You loved God. You are going to Heaven.'

She looked at him, with a hint of anger in her eyes and replied: 'How do you know?'

And he admitted he didn't. Nobody knows, pure and simple. It's just faith.

Failure and Achievement

My biggest achievement is, of course, Charlotte. If I was to pick one moment to describe as the best in my life, it would be around 4.25 am on April 6, 2006. Connie had called me to tell me they were taking her to theatre in the Rotunda Hospital. Half asleep, I asked her what I should do.

'Get here,' she said.

So I drove in at speed, parked, went in and identified my-self. I didn't get to see Connie. But I was brought to a room. A smallish room. It contained one chair. After half an hour or so, someone brought me a cup of tea and a couple of biscuits. I sat there for a couple of hours.

Nobody came near. Then, just before 4.30, the doors burst open. A couple of nurses were wheeling an incubator through the room.

'Is that...?' I began to ask.

'It's a girl,' she said. And off they went.

It was another twenty minutes before anyone came near. Just as well. I was weeping. Eventually, I got to see the baby and then Connie who was still in a lot of pain. It was nonetheless joyous.

As soon as 8.00 am passed, I began ringing our families, crying each time I broke the happy news. Nothing, no other day, compares.

Professionally, life wasn't so good. I was probably fired or shafted more often than anyone in history. Up to Number three in the *Herald*? Well, after the tragic Eastbourne Air Crash in 1984, it was back down to Number Three in the Features Department.

Number three in *The Star*? Well, when they all shagged off to the *Sunday World* and I *still* didn't get the top job – the *Indo* managing director Joe Hayes had the grace to apologise, saying it wasn't his call (!) – and I was shoved further and further down the pecking order when the *next* editor arrived (despite being told I had the gig on the Saturday prior to the announcement) and off to the *Tribune* at whose behest I will never know, but it certainly made some people happy!

And so I was appointed as editor of the *Tribune*. Glory Days? Well, no. Less than three years into the job I was a) removed as editor with a guarantee of holding on to my job and salary and b) fired. Off to the *Sunday World* and fired again. Strewth. I should get on to the Guinness Book of Records. But *do* let me say, I bear nobody any ill will. Such is life.

A World Without

One of the most difficult things to grasp about leaving this world is actually the fact that it will go on. Imagine that. A world functioning without Paddy Murray.

Is the Timing Your Choice?

My mother died at the age of 91, the year I turned 50. She hadn't been well from March so I visited her on a regular basis in her home in Dalkey. It was in the early summer, when she had recovered somewhat, that she asked me what I would be doing to celebrate my big five-oh which was on August 5. I am sure she fully expected me to say I was either a) heading to New York for a weekend with some mates – I was still allowed to fly at that time, or b) not doing much or c) having a big party which she no doubt would have offered to fund.

But I had already made my mind up. I would have my siblings and their partners around to what was for us our relatively new house.

In the following months, I visited my mother on an almost daily basis, probably more than 100 times. On each occasion – well, until maybe July when she spent most of her day sleeping – she would ask when the 'party' was. On each occasion, I would explain that it would be in early August as my birthday fell on the 5th. She was pleased as punch that the family would be together – we're close, but complete get togethers were rare – and that is was what I wanted.

And so, though she was unwell, the dinner party was arranged for the Saturday before my birthday the following Tuesday. It was a lovely evening, six of us, those with partners plus my niece, chatted away until about 1.30 am. And they left.

We found out the next day that was just about exactly when my mother died. Right then. Dinner party over. Mission accomplished. Family together.

I have told this story over and over again to a few raised eyebrows. Generally, the response is about a dad staying alive for a wedding, a granny staying alive until a Holy Communion has been completed or an uncle battling on until the nephew plays and wins in the big final.

One other odd thing. When I woke the next day my brother was at the door to tell me my mum had died. As soon as I closed the door, a caricature of my father by Bobby Pyke, which had appeared in a topical magazine, snapped its cord and fell to the ground. (You may hum the theme to the Twilight Zone here.)

My Favourite Word

There is one word which I discovered, late in life, is more important than any other in the English language. And that word is 'dad'. And it is important when spoken by my daughter. Because it is me she is addressing. It is me she is calling dad.

It is a word full of love, a word full of admiration, a word full of expectation. Oh, how she loves me and how I love her. How we admire each other. And how much we expect of each other. Well, she expects of me and I hope for her. I suppose that's more accurate. But that word, dad, when she says it my heart swells up. I almost cry every time. 'Dad, can you do this?' 'Dad, how do you say that word?' 'Dad, I'm hungry.' 'Dad, I love you.' One sentence no more important than the other. Because they all contain the word 'dad'.

Father's Day

Which brings me to Father's Day, 2014, Sunday, June 15th. The front of the card said: Happy Fathers' Day DADDY. Inside was a letter from Charlotte.

Dublin 6W June 2014

Dear Dad,

I love you so much because you spoil me. You are the greatest because you're funny.

I know you're sick but I still love you I know you sit on the sofa all day but I still love you. I know you're always busy but I still love you with all my heart because you're the greatest dad in the world!

From your only kid

CHARLOTTE!

And there was a poem.

Daddy I love you
For all that you do
I'll kiss you and hug you
'Cause you love me too
You feed me and need me
To teach you to play
So smile 'cause I love you
On this Fathers' Day

From Charlotte

Best present ever. And treasured forever. Even now.

She also had to write a short story to illustrate a drawing her teacher, Miss Coughlan, had given her. It showed a girl crying over a broken mug, a mug on which the word 'Dad' was emblazoned. This is the story.

It was Sunday 15ᵗʰ June, Fathers' Day, and I was buying a mug for Dad. I got this mug that said 'Dad' and it had a big love-heart around it for €6.00. When I was bringing it into the house, I got a big fright because a spider ran across the floor. I dropped the mug and it broke. My Mom bought another mug and I gave it to my Dad. The end.

Ten Things I Saw that Charlotte Will Never See

1. Bus conductors. Mostly, they just went about their business. They'd rattle their bag off coins and sell you a ticket dispensed from an amazing machine hanging from their shoulders. Some, though, were proper characters. They'd sing. They'd tell jokes. They'd talk loudly all the way from Mount Merrion to Dun Laoghaire. On the way from the city, the bus would often pull in at Donnybrook church opposite the CIÉ depot. And we'd sit and wait for ten minutes as the crew changed. That's what it was in those days. A crew. A driver (pilot) and conductor (air steward).

2. I don't know what Charlotte would make of rabbit's ears. They'd sit on top of the television and be twisted around every now and then in the hope of improving the picture quality from lousy to less lousy, from snowy to less snowy. And that was for *one* channel.

3. I'm not sure Charlotte has ever seen those bags of plain crisps with a little bag of salt in them. Or a Flash bar with the chewiest toffee ever. Or gobstoppers, the enormous hard, round balls of sweetness we much preferred to aniseed balls. Which she will probably never see either.

4. Nor would she know what a May procession is. We had them in Mount Merrion. Hundreds would walk through the various roads in the area and Mass would be said, or Benediction held at Greenabbey Road.

5. They talk of recycling – but long before the word was ever in common usage we had the milkman call every day to take our old empty glass milk bottles and replace them with new, full ones. He'd call to collect his money once a week.

6. You can see old *Top of the Pops* on various channels these days. But that can't replicate the excitement of Thursday evenings, waiting to see who'd be on. And if your favourite group was on, well, it was just heaven.

7. There was no shame back then ... in some classrooms (I never saw it in 'Rock by the way) you'd see a leather strap hanging on a nail near the teacher's desk. It wasn't for holding his trousers up...

8. 'Herald, Press or Mail.' That's what the newsvendors shouted in Dublin up to the early sixties. Then the *Mail* ceased publication. Then the *Evening Press*. And the *Herald* stopped coming out in the afternoons and dropped the word 'evening' from its title.

9. Extravision made a fortune, for a while, for its proprietor and, indeed, inventor, Richard Murphy. You'd queue to rent a video of a movie. But like televisions themselves, they became so cheap nobody rented. And so Extravision died.

10. There's a little hook on the top of a can these days. You pull it and the top comes off. Of course there's a little hook, you say, how else would you open a can? With a can opener! But they're probably only in museums now.

The Bucket Emptied

Things I did which could have been on my bucket list.

1. Walked on a 1,000 year old street, at Wood Quay, before the City destroyed its own history.

2. Got thanked personally by Elton John for a review of his concert in the King's Hall in Belfast on June 15, 1984.

3. Gate-crashed a Bowie 'secret' gig in the Cat Club in New York.

4. Visited Sir George Martin's Air studio on the island of Montserrat where Duran Duran recorded *Rio*, Dire Straits made *Brothers in Arms* and the Rolling Stones and Paul McCartney recorded.

5. Climbed Croagh Patrick.

6. Saw *Carmen* at the Roman amphitheatre in Verona.

7. Stood on the roof of the World Trade Centre in New York in 1980.

8. Went to two soccer world cups (1990 and 1994) and a rugby world cup (1995)

9. Visited 45 countries. Ireland, England, Scotland, Wales, France, Spain, Portugal, Italy, Austria, Switzerland, San Marino, The Vatican, Belgium, Holland, Germany, Poland, Romania, Yugoslavia, Macedonia, Turkey, Latvia, Lithuania, Estonia, Belarus, Russia, Sweden, Denmark, Yugoslavia, Albania, Slovenia, Malta, Liechtenstein, Thailand, India, Abu Dhabi, Singapore, Australia, Tunisia, South Africa, Syria, Canada, United States, Antigua, Montserrat, Bahamas.

10. And best of all, married Connie and, together, had Charlotte!

A Personal Achievement

I don't know that I achieved that much professionally in life. But there is a plaque on the wall of a building in Dublin and... no, it's not for me. But I got it put there.

I always wondered why there was no plaque on the old Adelphi Cinema on Middle Abbey Street commemorating the fact that it was the only place in Dublin The Beatles ever played. Yes, I know lots of other people played there too. But The Beatles are The Beatles.

So some time in 2017 I set about getting a plaque erected. I found out how it was done. Immediately, I was presented with an obstacle. The Adelphi frontage – now the exit from Arnott's car park – was a protected structure and a plaque could not be placed on it. Damn. I called an architect friend, John Mitchell.

'It's not the original frontage,' he said. 'It's facsimile.'

Obstacle cleared.

I contacted local Councillor Mary Freehill and she agreed to take the matter to the council's Commemorative Naming Sub Committee which decides these matters. It took a little time but it got through.

Now I was in the hands of Sean Deegan of Arnott's – their building, so they had to agree – and Jackie O'Reilly who was the Council official in charge of these matters. There was a discussion about the date of any unveiling. I would only accept one date: November 7 – 55 years to the day since the band played their two gigs in the Adelphi. And so that was agreed.

It was Gay Byrne's last public appearance, and though before he spoke he was hesitant and sounded weak, once he stood at the lectern he boomed with a strong voice and held the crowd spellbound for ten minutes. An absolute pro and a gentleman. It is a great source of pride that he did us all the honour of appearing, despite his health woes.

Journalist Éanna Brophy, who was there on the night, was at the unveiling, as was the garda on duty that night, Tom Butler. In attendance were Beatles fanatics from all over the place cheering. We then adjourned to a bar, appropriately The Adelphi, to sing a few Beatles songs. Now of that I *am* proud.

Kevin Street

The gardaí occupied some old buildings on Kevin Street for many years. Indeed, policemen of one sort or another occupied those buildings for 200 years. But when the local gardaí moved to their new building next door another unit moved into the old buildings and even erected a massive black gate to stop anyone looking in. Looking in at what? Well, at the almost 1,000 year old St Sepulchre's Palace, once home to the Archbishops of Dublin.

Part of those original buildings became the garda barracks and more is no doubt underground.

So I campaigned, almost alone, then Jason McElligot in Marsh's Library joined me. *The Irish Times* published two articles about the buildings, and eventually the Office of Public Works said, in writing, that when the gardaí moved out – which was expected to take place in 2022 – the buildings would revert to cultural usage. So they must.

Awards

I won the Young Journalist of the Year title in 1975. It was for an article about plans to build a marina in Scotsman's Bay in Dun Laoghaire, a plan opposed by many in the area.

I suppose the piece in the *Herald* was most notable for the headline *No, No, No Say Dun Laoghaire*, using the kind of appalling grammar which has become so familiar to us nowadays. The most memorable thing about the award ceremony was that when the winners posed with Minister Garret FitzGerald, he turned to me and asked:

'Eh, and what do you do?'

'I'm a journalist,' I replied, thinking that holding the Young Journalist of the Year Award might have been some kind of clue as to my occupation.

He was then and remained, as I realised in later meetings with him, a little bit of a featherhead. But also a genius, honest, decent and just very nice.

I won Popular Columnist of the Year in 2014. Looks like I'm due an award every 41 years or so!

Great Last Words

I think, perhaps, one of the most inspiring paragraphs I ever read, was in the *London Times* obituary of Val Doonican. And this is it:

> Doonican attributed his huge success as a television enter-tainer to a comment from his dying father. "You think I'm terrific don't you. Well before I die it's only fair to tell you I'm not. When I'm gone a lot of people will probably tell you that your dad was no good. Nothing will please me more than for you to say, 'Yes he told me that himself', Doonican recalled.

I know that some people didn't like me. I know that many thought me arrogant. I know lots thought I never shut up. And many others thought me a bit of an eejit. But there were some who liked me and a few who loved me. Well, they were *all* right.

But as long as my family loved me, I really don't care. I hated nobody and I loved many.

Thank you all.

A POSTSCRIPT ...

Top Twenty of Everything

My Favourite Albums

1. *Revolver*, The Beatles
2. *Beggar's Banquet*, The Rolling Stones
3. *Village Green Preservation Society*, The Kinks
4. *Illinois*, Sufjan Stevens
5. *Wilco*, Wilco
6. *Baldry's Out*, Long John Baldry
7. *Rubber Soul*, The Beatles
8. *Blind Faith*, Blind Faith
9. *Closing Time*, Tom Waits
10. *Dark Side of the Moon*, Pink Floyd
11. *Excitable Boy*, Warren Zevon
12. *Fin de Siècle*, Divine Comedy
13. *A Hard Day's Night*, The Beatles
14. *The Beatles (The White Album)*, The Beatles
15. *Infinite Arms*, Band of Horses
16. *In the Court of the Crimson King*, King Crimson
17. *Jackrabbit Slim*, Steve Forbert
18. *Led Zeppelin III*, Led Zeppelin
19. *Lou*, Joseph Arthur
20. *Life'll Kill Ya*, Warren Zevon

The Best Gigs

1. Fleetwood Mac, National Stadium, October 1969
2. Coldplay, Croke Park, July 2017

3. Leonard Cohen, Kilmainham, 2014

4. Bruce Springsteen, Slane, 1985

5. Warren Zevon, Olympia, 2000

6. Paul McCartney, RDS Dublin, 2010

7. Elbow, Olympia, 2017

8. U2, Slane, 2001

9. The Kinks, National Stadium, 1981

10. David Byrne, 3Arena, 2018

11. David Bowie, Hammersmith Odeon, 1973

12. Walking on Cars, Olympia, 2015

13. Peter Green Splinter Group, The Village Dublin, 2001

14. Joseph Arthur, Whelans, November 2016

15. Psychadelic Furs, Academy Dublin, 2017

16. Elton John, Belfast Kings Hall, 1984

17. Gordon Lightfoot, Stadium, 1974

18. James Taylor, Stadium, 1974

19. Neil Finn, Olympia, 2014

20. Flamin' Amy and Sweet Patata, Lynch's, Manhattan, 1994

My Favourite Books

1. *Puckoon* by Spike Milligan

2. *Oh The Places You'll Go* by Dr Seuss

3. *Love in the Time of Cholera* by Gabriel García Márquez

4. *The Choirboys* by Joseph Wambaugh

5. *Three Men in a Boat* by Jerome K. Jerome

6. *The Ascent of Rum Doodle* by W.E. Bowman

7. *Team of Rivals* by Doris Kearns Goodwin

8. *An tOileánach* by Tomás Ó Criomhthain

9. *Metamorphosis* by Franz Kafka

10. *Malone Dies* by Samuel Beckett

11. *The Third Policeman* by Flann O'Brien

12. *The Code of the Woosters* by P.G. Wodehouse

13. *Animal Farm* by George Orwell

14. *The Devil's in the Drum* by John Lucy

15. *A Clockwork Orange* by Anthony Burgess

16. *Fiche Blian ag Fás* by Muiris Ó Súileabháin

17. *One Day in the Life of Ivan Denisovich* by Solzhenitsyn

18. *Dubliners* by James Joyce

19. *To Kill a Mockingbird* by Harper Lee

20. *Catch 22* by Joseph Heller

The Top Twenty Songs*

1. 'Handbags and Gladrags' by Chris Farlowe

2. 'Turn! Turn! Turn!' by The Byrds

3. 'Waterloo Sunset' by The Kinks

4. '#9 Dream' by John Lennon

5. 'Old Town' by Philip Lynott

6. 'She's A Rainbow' by The Rolling Stones

7. 'Here in the Dark' by Aoife Nessa Francis

8. 'Since You've Been Gone' by Rainbow

9. 'Senza Una Donna' by Paul Young and Zucchero

10. 'Five Years' by David Bowie

11. 'For Your Love' by The Yardbirds

12. 'Hang on Sloopy' by The Real McCoys

13. 'Astronaut' by Liam Geddes

14. 'Across the Universe' by The Beatles

15. 'Dearg Doom' by Horslips

16. 'A Thrill's a Thrill' by Long John Baldry

17. 'Heydey' by Mic Christopher
18. 'Tenderness on the Block' by Warren Zevon
19. 'Carry It With You' by Niall Connolly
20. 'Christmas Past' by Mick Flannery

*(This list changes about every couple of hours)

My Favourite Movies

1. *Breakfast at Tiffany's*
2. *Withnail and I*
3. *The Thomas Crown Affair*
4. *West Side Story*
5. *It's a Mad Mad Mad Mad World*
6. *Being There*
7. *Adam and Paul*
8. *The Producers*
9. *Badlands*
10. *Kind Hearts and Coronets*
11. *Dr Strangelove*
12. *The Commitments*
13. *It's a Wonderful Life*
14. *Jean de Florette/Manon de Sources*
15. *Carry on Sergeant*
16. *The Great Escape*
17. *In Bruges*
18. *My Life as a Dog*
19. *Barry Lyndon*
20. *Johnny Got His Gun*

My Favourite Pubs in Dublin

(With apologies to the other 480 I visited but do not have space to list!)

1. Toners
2. Byrne's of Galloping Green
3. Brady's of Terenure
4. The Pearl Bar (closed)
5. The Oval, Abbey Street
6. The Palace Bar, Fleet Street
7. Peter's Pub, Johnston's Place
8. Mulligan's, Poolbeg Street
9. The Headline, Leonard's Corner
10. Ryan's, Parkgate Street
11. Whelan's, Camden Street
12. Ryan's, Camden Street
13. Higgins', Abbey Street (closed)
14. Kehoe's, South Anne Street
15. Valance and McGrath, North Wall Quay (closed)
16. The Toby Jug, South King Street (closed)
17. Grogan's, St William Street
18. Hogan's, Sth Great George's Street
19. The Princes, Princes Street (closed)
20. Bowe's, Fleet Street